SEPARATE TABLES

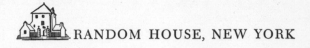RANDOM HOUSE, NEW YORK

SEPARATE TABLES

TWO PLAYS BY TERENCE RATTIGAN

To my mother

SEPARATE TABLES *was first presented by The Producers Theatre in association with Hecht-Lancaster at The Music Box, New York City, on October 25, 1956.*

Directed by Peter Glenville
Settings by Michael Weight
Lighting and Supervision by Paul Morrison
Production by arrangement with Stephen Mitchell

The action of both plays takes place in the Beauregard Hotel, Bournemouth. a seaside town on the south coast of England.

TABLE BY THE WINDOW

A Play in Three Scenes

TABLE BY THE WINDOW

(In Order of Speaking)

MABEL	Georgia Harvey
LADY MATHESON	Jane Eccles
MRS. RAILTON-BELL	Phyllis Neilson-Terry
MISS MEACHAM	May Hallatt
DOREEN	Helena Carroll
MR. FOWLER	William Podmore
MRS. SHANKLAND	Margaret Leighton
MISS COOPER	Beryl Measor
MR. MALCOLM	Eric Portman
CHARLES STRATTON	Donald Harron
JEAN TANNER	Ann Hillary

Time: Winter.

Scene 1—Dining Room. Dinner.

Scene 2—Lounge. After Dinner.

Scene 3—Dining Room. Breakfast.

Scene I

The dining room of the Beauregard Private Hotel, near Bournemouth. It is small, rather bare and quite unpretentious. A door at back
leads into the lounge, a swing door upstage right into the kitchen, and
another downstage right into the hall and the rest of the hotel. Windows left are curtained at the moment, for it is a winter evening, about
seven o'clock, and the guests are at dinner.

Each sits at a small separate table, except for a young couple,
CHARLES STRATTON and JEAN TANNER who, as mere transients, oc-
cupy a table together in a corner of the room, not garnished, as are the
other tables, with the bottles of medicine and favorite pickles and other
idiosyncratic personal accessories of the permanent residents. Surpris-
ingly, for they are an attractive-looking pair, CHARLES and JEAN are
paying no attention to each other at all, and each is avidly reading a
book propped up on the flower vase between them.

Prominently placed, and indeed a rather prominent-looking person
altogether, is MRS. RAILTON-BELL. All the ladies (except JEAN who
wears slacks) always change "into something" for dinner, but MRS.
RAILTON-BELL always changes into something much grander than the
others. All the ladies (except JEAN) wear fur stoles, but MRS. RAILTON-
BELL wears silver foxes. All the ladies (except JEAN) wear some small
items of jewelry, but MRS. RAILTON-BELL's are far less small than the others.

MISS MEACHAM sits near her, reading (very close to her unspectacled
eyes) a copy of Racing Up to Date. Although much the same age as
MRS. RAILTON-BELL (about sixty-five) she is dressed in a far more
sprightly fashion, but has not succeeded in looking any younger.

LADY MATHESON, a Civil Servant's widow, living on an annuity and
therefore the poorest of all the residents, sits close by, a gray-faced,

5

mousy, impeccably dressed woman, rather younger than the other two.
MR. FOWLER, *ex-public-school master, seventyish, quiet and impassive-looking, sits further away.*

The table by the window is unoccupied—as is another towards the center of the room and close to MRS. RAILTON-BELL.

*Two waitresses, one middle-aged (*MABEL*) the other young (*DOREEN*), serve the various tables.* MABEL *is taciturn, gloomy and dependable.* DOREEN *is flighty, talkative and undependable. At the moment only* MABEL *is visible. She is serving* LADY MATHESON.

MABEL

Were you stuffed pork or goulash?

LADY MATHESON

Stuffed pork.

MABEL

Sorry. I thought you were goulash.
(She stumps with the unwanted goulash to the kitchen door.)

LADY MATHESON

It was probably my fault.

MABEL
(Gloomily)
I dare say. *(She passes on to* MISS MEACHAM*)* Now, you *were* goulash, weren't you, Miss Meacham?

MISS MEACHAM
(Deep in her book)
What? Oh, yes, Mabel. Thank you.

MABEL
(*Serving her*)
And what to follow—the mousse angelic, or the turnover?

MISS MEACHAM
Which do you think?

MABEL
Turnover.

MISS MEACHAM
Turnover, then.
(MABEL *drifts away*.)

MRS. RAILTON-BELL
I think Cook's acquiring a little lighter touch with her pastry, don't you think?

MISS MEACHAM
Not judging by the tarts we had at tea yesterday. Cannon balls.

MRS. RAILTON-BELL
Did you think so? I quite liked them. I much preferred them to those pink cakes on Tuesday.

MISS MEACHAM
I didn't mind the pink cakes. The tarts gave me the collywobbles. I had the most terrible dreams.

MRS. RAILTON-BELL
(*With a faint smile*)
I thought you were always having dreams.

MISS MEACHAM

Oh, these weren't my proper dreams. Not the ones I make myself dream. (*After a slight pause*) I talked to Louis XV on Thursday night.

MRS. RAILTON-BELL

(*Plainly humoring her*)

Did you indeed, dear?

MISS MEACHAM

The goulash's rather good. I think you made a mistake.
(*She goes back to her book. There is a silence for a few moments while* MISS MEACHAM *peruses her* Racing Up to Date *with myopic concentration.*)

MRS. RAILTON-BELL

Think you've found a winner for tomorrow, Miss Meacham?

MISS MEACHAM

Well, according to this form book, Marston Lad is worth a bob or two each way.

MRS. RAILTON-BELL

I never bet nowadays. (*After a meditative pause*) When my husband was alive he used sometimes to put as much as five pounds on a horse for me.

MISS MEACHAM

(*Looking up*) I used to bet on ponies when my father was alive and I had an allowance.
(*She goes back to her* Racing Up to Date.)

8

MRS. RAILTON-BELL

(*Suddenly irritable*)

Why don't you get spectacles?

(MISS MEACHAM *lowers her book.*)

MISS MEACHAM

Because I don't need them.

(*She goes back to her book again.* DOREEN, *the other waitress, has come in and is now hovering over* MR. FOWLER.)

DOREEN

Sorry, Mr. Fowler, the goulash's off.

(MR. FOWLER *looks up abstractedly.*)

MR. FOWLER

What? Oh. What about the cold pie?

DOREEN

I shouldn't have that, if I were you. I saw what went into it. If I were you I'd have the tongue—

MR. FOWLER

All right. Whatever you say.

(DOREEN *disappears into the kitchen.*)

MRS. RAILTON-BELL

(*To* LADY MATHESON, *meaningly*)

She won't last.

LADY MATHESON

I'm afraid not.

MRS. RAILTON-BELL

Still, it's disgraceful that the goulash's off, and two people not even in yet.

LADY MATHESON

I know.

MRS. RAILTON-BELL

Of course Mr. Malcolm's never on time (*She indicates the table by the window*) and really deserves it. (*In another confidential whisper*) Anyway, after those long sessions at the Feathers, I often wonder if he ever really knows what he's eating. But the new lady (*She indicates the other unoccupied table*)—I mean, my dear, what will she think?

LADY MATHESON

I saw her arrive.

MRS. RAILTON-BELL

Did you?

LADY MATHESON

Did you?

MRS. RAILTON-BELL
(*Slightly annoyed*)

I was in the lounge, but I didn't—excuse me—think it quite the thing to peer out of the window at her—

LADY MATHESON
(*Firmly*)

I happened to be in the hall.

MISS MEACHAM

I met her on the stairs.

MRS. RAILTON-BELL

Really, dear?

MISS MEACHAM

(*Still absorbed in her book*)

She's called Mrs. Shankland. She comes from London, she arrived by train, she has four suitcases and a hatbox and she's staying two weeks.

MRS. RAILTON-BELL

(*Unwillingly impressed*)

Four suitcases?

MISS MEACHAM

And a hatbox.

LADY MATHESON

She was awfully smartly dressed. Nothing flashy—very good taste —but—well—Mayfair, if you know what I mean.

MRS. RAILTON-BELL

Really? (*Changing the subject from this unwelcome topic*) It was quite nice out this afternoon, didn't you think, dear—I mean, for December?

LADY MATHESON

I didn't go out, I'm afraid. There was a Sibelius concert on the Home—

MRS. RAILTON-BELL

You and your music. Did you go out, Mr. Fowler?

MR. FOWLER

What? No, I didn't. I was waiting for a telephone call.

MRS. RAILTON-BELL

I was the only brave one then? Fancy.

(*She breaks off abruptly as the door from the hall opens and* MRS. SHANKLAND—ANNE—*the new arrival, comes in. She is about forty, and, as she stands just inside the room looking around rather timidly, she seems entirely out of place in such an environment. Not that her clothes are unsuitable, although they are smart, nor that her coiffure is too stylish, although it is stylish, but that she has brought on with her an air of Belgravia and the smarter London restaurants. She stands now as if waiting for a headwaiter to guide her to her table. None of the other guests glance at her.* MABEL, *who is serving* MISS MEACHAM *with her turnover, turns and sees her.*)

MABEL

You're the new one, aren't you?

ANNE

Yes.

MABEL

You're here.

(*She points to the table in the center.*)

ANNE

Oh. Thank you.

(*She goes to the table and sits down. Dead silence still reigns.* MABEL *hands her a menu, and while she is studying it, eyes begin to cast quick, furtive glances in her direction.*)

MABEL

The brown windsor or the *petite marmite*?

ANNE

I don't think I'll have any soup, thank you. I'll try the goulash.

MABEL

That's right. We've got a portion left.
(MR. FOWLER *glares furiously at* MABEL *as she goes past him to the kitchen, but decides not to make a scene. Eyes are lowered again as* ANNE *looks curiously round the room. The silence continues until it is at length broken by* MRS. RAILTON-BELL, *speaking now in a rather louder and more self-consciously well-bred voice than before.*)

MRS. RAILTON-BELL

(*To* LADY MATHESON)
I was saying about the weather in December—

LADY MATHESON

Oh, yes?

MRS. RAILTON-BELL

It can be so treacherous, especially here, on the south coast. This afternoon, for instance, even though the sun was quite bright, I put on a fur coat—my warmest one too—the Persian lamb.

LADY MATHESON

Very sensible of you.
(*The two young people rise abruptly and make for the lounge door, each carrying their book. They have still, as far as we can see, not addressed a word to each other.* MRS. RAILTON-BELL *eyes them with disdain.*)

MRS. RAILTON-BELL

Trousers at dinner!

13

LADY MATHESON

I know.

MRS. RAILTON-BELL

And *he* never changes either. I wonder Miss Cooper doesn't say something. You'd think they'd teach them better manners at Oxford.

LADY MATHESON

Yes, you would. (*After a slight pause*) My husband was at Oxford.

MRS. RAILTON-BELL

(*Gently*)

Yes, dear. You've told me so before. Mine only went to Birmingham because of the wonderful engineering course they have there. He hated it, of course.

(MISS COOPER *has come in and is crossing the room towards* ANNE. *She is youngish, with a rather masculine appearance and a quiet manner.*)

MISS COOPER

Good evening, Mrs. Railton-Bell.

MRS. RAILTON-BELL

Good evening, Miss Cooper.

MISS COOPER

Good evening, Lady Matheson.

LADY MATHESON

Good evening.

(MISS MEACHAM *does not look up.* MISS COOPER *continues her journey towards* ANNE'S *table.*)

MISS COOPER

Is everything all right, Mrs. Shankland?

ANNE

Yes, thank you.

MISS COOPER

I'm so sorry I wasn't there to show you your table. I had a telephone call from London. Are you being looked after all right?

ANNE

Yes, thank you.
(MABEL *has brought her dish and now places it before her.*)

MISS COOPER
(*Sharply*)

No soup?

ANNE

No. I don't care for it. It's bad for the figure.

MISS COOPER

I should't have thought you'd have to worry about that, Mrs. Shankland.

ANNE

Oh, I do. I work at modeling, you know.

MISS COOPER

And now you're down here for a little rest?

ANNE

Yes. That's right.

MISS COOPER

I hope you find your room quite comfortable.

ANNE

I'm sure I shall.

MISS COOPER

If there's anything you want, please don't hesitate to ask me.

ANNE

I won't.
(MISS COOPER *flashes her a cordial smile, extinguished instantly as she turns away. She glances at the empty table by the window, and summons* MABLE *with a gesture.*)

MISS COOPER

Mabel, go to Mr. Malcolm's room and tell him—

MABEL

I've been. He's not there.

MISS COOPER

Oh. Have they kept something hot for him?

MABEL

Yes, but Cook says if he's not in in five minutes he'll have to have cold.

MISS COOPER

Oh, well, I don't expect he'll be more than that.
(MABLE *looks unconvinced.* MISS COOPER *goes towards the hall door.* MR. FOWLER, *rising from his table, intercepts her.*)

MR. FOWLER

Did I hear you say something about a telephone call?

MISS COOPER

I'm afraid it wasn't from your guest, Mr. Fowler. It was from Major Pollock. He wanted to leave a new forwarding address.

MRS. RAILTON-BELL

Ringing up from London? That's very extravagant—for the Major—

MISS COOPER

(*With a faint smile*)

He was calling from a friend's house, I gather. He's coming back next Tuesday, he says.

MISS MEACHAM

(*Through her book*)

Oh, God! That old bore!

MR. FOWLER

I can't understand Philip not ringing up. How can he expect to be met at the station if we don't know what train—

MISS COOPER

Have you tried ringing him?

MR. FOWLER

Yes. Twice. No answer either time. Perhaps I'd better try again—
(*He goes through the change in his pocket.*)

MISS COOPER

It's a little late, Mr. Fowler. There's only one train left from London—

MR. FOWLER

(*On his way to the door*)

Please don't worry about the room, Miss Cooper. If anything's gone wrong—which I don't believe, mind you—I'll pay for it, I promise you.

MISS COOPER

That won't be necessary, Mr. Fowler. But I *would* rather like to know—if you don't mind—as soon as possible—

(MR. FOWLER *goes*. MISS COOPER *takes up the vase from his table*.)

MRS. RAILTON-BELL

(*Sympathetically*)

It's too bad, Miss Cooper. This is the third time, isn't it?

MISS COOPER

I expect he'll turn up. Just forgotten to phone, that's all. You know what these Bohemian young people are like.

(*She goes out*.)

MRS. RAILTON-BELL

(*To* LADY MATHESON)

I don't, as it happens. I don't care for Bohemians. (*In her confidential whisper*) We have one too many here, I should have thought. (*With her head she indicates the table by the window*) And I'm beginning to doubt the very existence of Mr. Fowler's famous young painter friend.

LADY MATHESON

I know he exists. Mr. Fowler showed me an article on him in *Picture Post*. He was the head boy of Mr. Fowler's house at Tonbridge, I gather. So proud of him, Mr. Fowler is—it's really quite touching to hear him go on—

MRS. RAILTON-BELL

Well, I think it's a disgrace that he keeps on letting him down like this—

(MISS MEACHAM *suddenly closes her book.*)

MISS MEACHAM

Nonsense.

MRS. RAILTON-BELL

(*Startled*)

What, dear?

MISS MEACHAM

It's not a disgrace at all. Why should we old has-beens expect the young to show us consideration? We've had our life. They've still got theirs to live. Seeing us can only remind them of death, and old people's diseases. I've got two of the prettiest nieces you ever saw. You've seen their photographs in my room. But they never come near me, and I wouldn't like it if they did. God knows I don't want to remind them of what they've got to become.

(*She goes into the lounge, holding her book.*)

MRS. RAILTON-BELL

(*In her confidential whisper to* LADY MATHESON)

I'm getting a little worried about Miss Meacham.

LADY MATHESON

She's certainly getting more and more—unusual, every day.

MRS. RAILTON-BELL

These dream games of hers. Well, I suppose they're harmless—but I really don't know what a psychiatrist would say. The human mind, you know—it's a very delicate piece of machinery—as my husband used to say—and—one never knows. Well— (*She rises majestically*) Shall I see you in the lounge, or have you a date with the Third Programme?

LADY MATHESON

No. There's nothing worth hearing on tonight.

MRS. RAILTON-BELL

Good. *A tout à l'heure,* then.

(*She sweeps regally into the lounge.* LADY MATHESON *is now on her sweet.* ANNE *has finished toying with her goulash. Deep silence reigns.* MABEL *comes in*).

MABEL

(*To* ANNE)

I've brought you the turnover. It's better than the other.

ANNE

Oh. Thank you so much.

(MABEL *replaces her dishes and goes out. Once more silence reigns. The door is pushed open rather violently and* JOHN MALCOLM *comes in. He is in the early forties, of rather rugged appearance, untidily dressed, and with unruly hair. When he speaks it will be with a slight north country accent. He looks quickly at his watch, and then at the kitchen door. Then he walks towards the table by the window. To reach it he has to pass* ANNE. *She has seen him before he sees her, and is now staring at him, remotely, with no change of expression. Conscious of the stare, he looks in her direction and then stops dead, his back to the audience. After a moment he walks on to his own table and takes his seat, which is facing hers. He stares at the tablecloth.* DOREEN *comes in.*)

DOREEN

Oh. You in at last? Thank heavens. I thought we'd never get off. Where you been? The Feathers?

JOHN

Yes.

DOREEN

Thought so. The goulash's off. You'll have to have stuffed pork.

JOHN

(Still staring at the tablecloth)

That's all right.

DOREEN

Brown windsor, like usual?

JOHN

Yes.

> (DOREEN *goes. There is silence among the three. Finally* LADY MATHESON *finishes, gets up, and goes out into the lounge, as* DOREEN *comes in with* JOHN'S *soup.*)

DOREEN

There you are. Tuck into that. Not but what I wouldn't expect you've had enough liquid tonight already.

> (*She goes out.* JOHN *crumbles a piece of bread, and then slowly lifts his eyes from the tablecloth to gaze at the other guest.*)

JOHN

(At length)

Is this coincidence?

ANNE

Of course.

JOHN

What are you doing here?

ANNE

A rest cure.

JOHN

Why this place—of all places?

ANNE

It was recommended to me.

JOHN

Who by?

ANNE

A man I met at a party somewhere.

JOHN

He didn't tell you I was here?

ANNE

He did say something about a journalist—called John Malcolm. Is that you?

JOHN

Yes.

ANNE

John Malcolm. Oh, yes, of course. Your Christian names.

JOHN

(*Savagely*)

Why, for the love of God, didn't you go to the Royal Bath or the Norfolk or the Branksome Towers, or any of the grand hotels—why?

(*He stops as* DOREEN *comes in.*)

DOREEN

What you having after, 'cause Cook's got to leave it out. Turnover is best.

JOHN

All right.

DOREEN

Finished your soup?

JOHN

Yes, thank you.

DOREEN

You haven't touched it. I *said* too much liquid—

(*She takes the soup into the kitchen.*)

ANNE

I couldn't afford a grand hotel.

JOHN

He pays you alimony, doesn't he?

ANNE

Seven fifty a year. I don't find it very easy. You see, I'm not getting work these days—

JOHN

I thought he was a rich man.

ANNE

Michael? Oh, no. His antique shop lost a lot of money.

JOHN

He gets his name in the papers a lot.

ANNE

Oh, yes. Quite a social figure—first nights and all that.

JOHN

How long exactly were you married to him?

ANNE

Three years and six months.

JOHN

Beating me by three months? I saw the headlines of the case. They were quite juicy—but not as juicy as ours—you'll admit. It was cruelty again, wasn't it?

ANNE

Yes.

JOHN

Did *he* try to kill you too?

ANNE
(*Quietly*)

No.

  (DOREEN *comes in with* JOHN's *second course.*)

DOREEN

There you are. Usual veg? (JOHN *nods*. DOREEN *helps him*) You look a bit down in the dumps tonight. Anything the matter?

JOHN

No.

DOREEN

All right. Don't take long, will you? My friend's waiting—
(*She goes out.* JOHN *makes no attempt to touch his food.*)

JOHN

How did he show *his* cruelty?

ANNE

In a lot of ways. Small ways. They can all be summed up by saying that he doesn't really like women.

JOHN

Why did he marry you?

ANNE

He wanted a wife.

JOHN

And you wanted a husband? (*She nods*) As wide a contrast as possible from your first, I suppose. Still, couldn't you have done a bit better for yourself?

ANNE

I suppose so. But he was gentle and kind and made me laugh and I was fond of him. I went into it with my eyes well open. I thought I could make it work. I was wrong. (JOHN *laughs suddenly*) What's the joke?

JOHN

A nice poser for a woman's magazine. Girls, which husband would you choose? One who loves you too little—or one who loves you too much? (*After a pause*) Third time lucky perhaps.

ANNE

Perhaps.
    (*Pause.*)

JOHN

How long are you staying here?

ANNE

I booked for two weeks.

JOHN

I'll go to London.

ANNE

No. If you feel like that, then I'll go to another hotel.

JOHN

That might be easier.
    (*Pause.*)

ANNE

John—I don't see why—

JOHN

Do you think these old women don't notice anything? They spend their whole days gossiping. It would take them less than a day to nose out the whole story and wouldn't they have a time with it! They're suspicious enough of me as it is. They know I write in the *New Outlook* under the name of Cato—and how they found that out I'll never know, because none of them would sully their dainty fingers by even touching such a bolshie rag.

26

ANNE

I read it every week.

JOHN

Turning left wing in your old age?

ANNE

(*Quietly*)

My old age?

JOHN

How old are you now?

ANNE

Well—let's just say eight years older than when I last saw you.

JOHN

Yes. You don't look it.

ANNE

Thank you. But I feel it.
  (*Pause.*)

JOHN

Why didn't you come to see me in prison yourself?

ANNE

I wanted to. I was stopped.

JOHN

Who by?

ANNE

My mother and father.

JOHN

I suppose they told you I might try to strangle you in front of the warder. I nearly did try to strangle your solicitor.

ANNE

They thought it would make it easier for you if I kept away.

JOHN

A very well-bred, Christian thought. My dear ex-in-laws. How are they?

ANNE

My father's dead. My mother lives in a place rather like this, in Kensington.
(*Pause.* JOHN *is gazing at her intently.*)

JOHN
(*At length*)
Then you'll go tomorrow, will you?

ANNE

Yes.

JOHN

Thank you. (*Stiffly*) I'm sorry to have to put you to so much inconvenience.

ANNE

That's all right.
(*He gets up abruptly from his table and walks up to hers.* ANNE *rises quickly.*)

JOHN

Well, what do we do—shake hands?

ANNE

I'm very glad to see you again, John.
(*She kisses him gently on the cheek.*)

JOHN

It may seem boorish of me not to be able to say the same, Anne. But then I am a boor, as you know. In fact, you must still have a scar on the side of your head to prove it to you.

ANNE

It's gone now.

JOHN

Gone? After five stitches and a week in hospital?

ANNE

Eight years will cure most scars.

JOHN

Most, I suppose. Not all, though. Well, good night.
(*He goes towards the hall door. Before he reaches it* MISS COOPER *comes in.*)

MISS COOPER

Mrs. Shankland— (*Seeing* JOHN) Oh, good evening, Mr. Malcolm.

JOHN

Good evening.
(*He makes to move past her.*)

MISS COOPER

Did you want something? Is there anything I can do for you?

JOHN

I've finished, thank you. I'm going out.

MISS COOPER

Oh. (*With a hint of anxiety*) It's a horrible night, you know. It's started to pour—

JOHN

It doesn't matter—
(*He goes into the hall.*)

MISS COOPER

(*Following him*)

I'll have to open the door for you. I've already locked up. Excuse me, Mrs. Shankland— (*She follows him out.* ANNE, *left alone, sits down again. She looks thoughtfully at herself in a hand mirror for a long time.* MISS COOPER *comes back*) Coffee is served in the lounge, Mrs. Shankland. I thought, when you've finished your dinner, you might like me to take you in there and introduce you to some of your fellow-guests. People are sometimes so odd about not talking to newcomers, I don't know why, and I hate any of my guests to feel lonely. (*Conversationally*) Loneliness is a terrible thing, don't you agree?

ANNE

Yes, I do agree. A terrible thing.
(*She gets up from the table.*)

MISS COOPER

Oh. Have you finished? Good. Then let's go in, shall we? The lounge is through here.
(*She leads the way to the lounge door.*)

ANNE

Thank you.

The Lights Fade

Scene II

The lounge, about two hours later. The dining room door is upstage right and the door leading to the hall is at back. French windows left are curtained, and we can hear the rain beating against them. There is a fireplace downstage right with an electric fire burning.

CHARLES *and* JEAN *are the only two residents in the room. They sit side by side on a sofa, still reading intently. Both are making an occasional note.*

CHARLES

(Breaking a long silence, into his book)

There's going to be a storm.

JEAN

Hell. I hate spray.

CHARLES

(After another silence)

Where are they all?

JEAN

The new one's gone up to her room. So has old Dream Girl. The Bournemouth Belle and Minnie Mouse are in the television room. Karl Marx is out boozing. Mr. Chips is still ringing up his painter friend.

CHARLES

He won't come.

JEAN

Of course he won't. (*She closes her book and stretches herself*) I've
finished my Stubbs. How are you doing with your anatomy?

CHARLES

I'd do better if you'd shut up.

JEAN

(*Going to the window*)

I didn't start the small talk. You did. Does your father know about
me?

CHARLES

(*Making a note*)

Yes.

JEAN

What did you tell him?

CHARLES

What?
(*She pushes his book against his lap, preventing him from reading.*)

JEAN

What did you tell him?

CHARLES

Don't do that, Jean. I'm in the middle of the trickiest duct in the
whole human body.

JEAN

What did you tell him?

CHARLES

(*Angrily*)

Oh, for God's sake—that we were in love with each other and were going to get married.

(*He pulls the book back and furrows his brows over it again.*)

JEAN

You told him a dirty lie, then, didn't you—I mean about us going to get married?

CHARLES

What? Oh, yes. I had to put it like that. Otherwise he wouldn't have understood. Now shut up, for God's sake.

JEAN

You'd better stop now. If you go on much longer you know you won't sleep and it'll make you old before your time.

(*He allows her to take the book from him.*)

CHARLES

I suppose you're right. Don't lose the place. (*He stretches*) My God —to be old before one's time. What a fate! I wonder if all old people are as miserable as these.

JEAN

They're not miserable. Look at old Dream Girl. She's as happy as a sandgirl communing with her spirits and waiting for the racing results. The Bournemouth Belle's quite happy, too, queening it around here in her silver fox, and with her daughter to look after her.

CHARLES

Has she got a daughter?

33

JEAN

Don't you listen to anything? She never stops trilling away about her dear Sibyl, and how they're really more like good pals than mother and daughter, and how dear Sibyl can't live without her—

CHARLES

You mean the daughter lives with her here? My God, what a fate! I haven't seen her—

JEAN

She's escaped for a couple of weeks, I gather, to an aunt. Anyway, the Bournemouth Belle's too self-centered an old brute to be anything but happy. Minnie Mouse *is* a bit gray and depressed, I grant. But she's got her music, and Mr. Chips has got his ex-pupils, even if he doesn't ever see them. As for Karl Marx—well—

CHARLES

Now you can't say Karl Marx isn't miserable. I've never seen a more miserable-looking wreck—

JEAN

Oh, I don't know. He's got his booze and his articles in the *New Outlook* and his vague air of a murky past, and his hints of former glories. (*With seriousness*) No, Charles. Do you know who I think is the only one in this hotel who really *is* miserable?

CHARLES

Miss Cooper?

JEAN

(*Scornfully*)

Miss Cooper? No. She's as gay as a bee pinning up her notices in the bathroom and being generally managerial. No. I meant the new one.

34

CHARLES

Mrs. Shankland? But you've only met her for a second an hour ago.

JEAN

A woman can't fool another woman with a pretty dress and a gay manner and a bright smile. She's been through some form of hell, that creature. Anyway, what's she doing down here? Dressed like that and looking like that she ought to be at the Royal Bath, or somewhere— (*Darkly*) Besides—she's not wearing a wedding ring.

CHARLES

Really, Jean, you're getting as bad as the old girls. Perhaps it's got broken or something.

JEAN

She's divorced—that I'm sure of.

CHARLES

Well, all right. So she's divorced. Does that make her a tragic figure? I should have thought, according to your ideas on marriage, it ought to make her a happy one.

JEAN

My ideas on marriage are only for us, Charles—because I'm going to have a career and you're going to be a famous surgeon and don't want hordes of children cluttering up your consulting room. But most people aren't as sensible as we are. They get married and are miserable when it goes wrong. Thank heavens that can't happen to us. We're too integrated. At least I am, I know, and I hope you are too—

CHARLES

Come and give me a kiss and I'll show you how integrated I am.

JEAN

I'd only put lipstick on your collar and the old girls will notice.

CHARLES

Sometimes, Jean darling, I'm not sure I wouldn't like to see you, just ever so slightly, disintegrate. (*He strides over and kisses her. She appears quite to enjoy the embrace. There is the sound of voices in the hall*) Oh, blast!

JEAN
(*Levelly*)

Wipe your mouth.

CHARLES

Damn it all, even the old girls know the facts of life.

JEAN

They may know them, but they don't like them.
(MRS. RAILTON-BELL *and* LADY MATHESON *come in.*)

MRS. RAILTON-BELL

Yes, wasn't he splendid? He completely floored that horrid socialist —(*Coldly*) Hullo. Finished your work?

CHARLES

Yes.

Together

JEAN

Yes we have. Just going to bed.

MRS. RAILTON-BELL

Good night.

36

CHARLES

Good night, Mrs. Railton-Bell.

} *Together*

JEAN

Good night, Lady Matheson.
(*They go out.*)

MRS. RAILTON-BELL

They've been making love.

LADY MATHESON

How do you know?

MRS. RAILTON-BELL

The look in their eyes. And just as I came in he was putting a handkerchief away with lipstick marks on it.

LADY MATHESON

Well, perhaps they *are* in love. I always thought there must be something.

MRS. RAILTON-BELL

But they're supposed to have come here just to work. Old friends, and all that. That's what they told Miss Cooper. If they're in love, why don't they say so? I hate anything furtive. What were we saying?
(*They take their—evidently usual—seats by the fire.*)

LADY MATHESON

About the man on television being so good.

MRS. RAILTON-BELL

Oh, yes. Now what was it he said that was so true— (*The French windows are opened from the outside and the curtains are blown violently*

37

inward) Good gracious! (*After a moment's battling with the bellying curtains,* JOHN *emerges. He is wearing a drenched raincoat*) Please close that at once. There's the most terrible draught.

JOHN

A draught? Oh, yes.

(*He disappears behind the curtains again.* MRS. RAILTON-BELL *exchanges a speaking glance with* LADY MATHESON *and frames word "drunk" with her lips.*)

LADY MATHESON

Yes. Now, what was it he said? So telling. Something about the national cake.

(JOHN'S *struggles to close the French windows are concluded. He emerges again and, still in his mackintosh, walks over to a chair by the fire, where he warms his hands. The two ladies look at him, and* MRS. RAILTON-BELL *decides to ignore his presence.*)

MRS. RAILTON-BELL

Yes. I remember now. It was in that wonderful answer he gave about leveling up rather than leveling down. He said, don't you remember, that whereas the socialists were only concerned about cutting the national cake into exactly equal slices, the Conservatives were trying to increase the size of the cake. (*She glances at* JOHN *to see if this has registered. Still holding his hands to the fire he does not appear to have heard*) And then he said that every wage increase meant a smaller cake for cutting—

JOHN
(*Abruptly*)

Who said this?

MRS. RAILTON-BELL

Sir Roger Williamson, on television.

JOHN

I might have guessed it.

MRS. RAILTON-BELL

(*Bristling*)

I gather you don't agree with what he said, Mr. Malcolm?

JOHN

Of course I don't agree. You know damn well I don't agree. That's not the point. They've got some clever people in that party. Why do they have to put an old ass like that on television—with a falsetto voice, a face like an angry walrus and the mind of a backward child of eight?

MRS. RAILTON-BELL

That was *not our* impression of Sir Roger.

(JOHN *does not reply. He seems, for the moment, to be lost in reverie.*)

JOHN

Poor old Roger. I suppose he needs the dough to make a little back on what he spends on all those girl friends of his.

MRS. RAILTON-BELL

(*After a moment's appalled silence*)

Do I understand that you are personally acquainted with Sir Roger, Mr. Malcolm?

(JOHN *turns and looks at her, as if, for the moment, he had been oblivious of her presence.*)

JOHN

No. Never met him.

MRS. RAILTON-BELL

Then may I ask by what right—

JOHN

No right. I just hear things, that's all.

MRS. RAILTON-BELL

Some very libelous things, if I may say so.

JOHN

Yes, the greater the truth the greater the libel is the phrase, isn't it? What else did Sir Roger say? Did he mention the go-slow in the docks?

MRS. RAILTON-BELL

Yes. As a matter of fact, he did. He said that the dock workers seemed to have no sense of national responsibility—

JOHN

There's no body of men in England with more.

MRS. RAILTON-BELL

That's no doubt something else that you have *heard*, Mr. Malcolm.

JOHN

No. That's something I *know*. I used to be a docker myself.
  (*Pause.*)

MRS. RAILTON-BELL

(*At length*)

I am not, if I may say so, at all surprised to hear it.

JOHN

And I am not surprised you're not surprised, Mrs. Railton-Bell. (*He burps gently*) Excuse me. Too much whisky. (*He sits down, still in his mackintosh.* MRS. RAILTON-BELL *and* LADY MATHESON *exchange a glance;* JOHN *intercepts it*) Keeps the cold out, you know. I gather you two ladies read the *New Outlook?*

MRS. RAILTON-BELL

I certainly never do any such thing. I wouldn't soil my hands—

JOHN

That's just what I thought. Do you, Lady Matheson?

LADY MATHESON

I have glanced at it on occasions, yes. (*Hastily*) Not for the political side, of course, but it has very good music criticism.

JOHN

So it was you who found out I was Cato, was it? Smart of you. How did you guess?

LADY MATHESON

(*Confused*)

If you must know, you left some typescript lying about on that table over there. I picked it up, not knowing what it was, and read just the opening paragraph, no more, but it was enough for me to recognize it in print a week or so later.

JOHN

I see. My fault then. No ill-feelings—on this side anyway. (*He burps again*) Excuse me. What was the article on?

LADY MATHESON

Dividends and wages.

JOHN

Did you read it all?

LADY MATHESON

Yes, I did.

JOHN

What did you think of it?

LADY MATHESON

(*With unusual spirit*)

Since you ask, I thought it was monstrous—utterly monstrous. I very nearly wrote you a letter about it.

JOHN

I wish you had. I enjoy controversy. You must have taken it a bit personally, I'm afraid.

LADY MATHESON

And how else could I take it? Do you realize that I have to live on a little less than half of what the average dock worker makes a year? My husband was in the Civil Service and died before the pension scheme came into force. Still, the sum he left me seemed perfectly adequate at the time. And now—

JOHN

I know. You can't afford to have your wireless repaired—and you live by it. You had to move into a small back room when they raised the hotel prices last year. You can only afford one cinema a week, in the front rows. I bet you don't even buy the *New Outlook*—you borrow it. In short, by any reasonable standards you're well below the poverty line, and, as the poor have always had my passionate sympathy, Lady Matheson, you have mine.

LADY MATHESON

Thank you, but I can do very well without it.

JOHN

I wonder if you can. You're the unlucky victims of our revolution—you and Miss Meacham and Mr. Fowler and the others. You should appeal to our humane instincts, Lady Matheson.

LADY MATHESON

By voting for your side, I suppose.

JOHN

That would be the most practical way, I agree.

LADY MATHESON
(Staunchly)

Never. Never till I die.

MRS. RAILTON-BELL

Tell me, why didn't you mention *me* just now, when you were talking of victims?

JOHN

Because you're not one, and won't be, either, until our capital levy gets at that tidy little nest egg of yours.

MRS. RAILTON-BELL
(Utterly outraged. To LADY MATHESON*)*

I think we should go, Gladys, and leave Mr. Malcolm down here to sleep it off.

 (The two ladies rise.)

JOHN

Oh, are you leaving, ladies? I mustn't forget my manners, must I?
(*He gets out of the chair, with slight difficulty*) I've enjoyed our little
chat. Don't forget, next election—vote Labour.

MRS. RAILTON-BELL

It's our own fault, Gladys. We should never have allowed ourselves
to be drawn into an argument with a drunken red. (*She has plainly in-
tended this as an exit line, but her exit is delayed because* LADY MATHE-
SON *is feverishly searching the room for something. Impatiently*)
Come along, Gladys.

LADY MATHESON

I've left my reading glasses somewhere.
(MISS COOPER *comes in with a tray on which is a coffee pot and
a cup.*)

MISS COOPER
(*Brightly*)
Here you are, Mrs. Railton-Bell. I'm not too late, I hope.

MRS. RAILTON-BELL
(*With heavy meaning*)
Thank you, Miss Cooper, but I'm not having my coffee tonight. (*Im-
patiently, to* LADY MATHESON) Can't you find them, dear?

LADY MATHESON

I'll just have another look in my chair.
(*She goes to her chair.* MISS COOPER *meanwhile has quickly
taken in the scene. She puts the tray down and she stares coldly
at* JOHN.)

44

MISS COOPER

(*In a very managerial voice*)
Mr. Malcolm, did you come in through the French windows?

JOHN

(*Humbly*)
Yes, I did.

MISS COOPER

You know that there's a hotel rule against that?

JOHN

I'd forgotten it. I'm very sorry.

MISS COOPER

There's mud all over the floor (*Advancing on his chair*) and you've been sitting in this chair with your wet mackintosh on. Oh, really!

JOHN

I'm very sorry.

MISS COOPER

I must ask you if you would be so kind as to take your mackintosh off and hang it up in the proper place. Also to wipe your shoes on the mat provided for that purpose.

JOHN

Yes. I'm very sorry.
(*He goes past* MRS. RAILTON-BELL *and out into the hall.* LADY MATHESON *is still looking in her chair.*)

MISS COOPER
(*Anxiously*)
Has there been a little bother?

MRS. RAILTON-BELL

A little bother is a distinct understatement.

MISS COOPER

Oh, dear! What was it?

MRS. RAILTON-BELL

I would prefer not to discuss it now. (*Very impatiently*) For heaven's sake, come along, Gladys. That dreadful man may be back at any moment.

LADY MATHESON
(*Triumphantly*)
Ah. I've got them. They were underneath the chair.

MRS. RAILTON-BELL

I can't think why you didn't look there in the first place.

LADY MATHESON

Well, I was sitting in Mr. Fowler's chair after dinner, you see, as the new lady was sitting in mine, quite inadvertently, I'm sure, and I thought—

MRS. RAILTON-BELL

It doesn't matter, dear. Go along now. Quick. (*She shoos her through the door and turns to* MISS COOPER) I should like to see you tomorrow morning after breakfast, Miss Cooper. Good night.

MISS COOPER

Good night, Mrs. Railton-Bell.

(MRS. RAILTON-BELL *goes out.* MISS COOPER *sighs and goes over to the chair in which* JOHN *has sat. She takes the cushion out and places it near the fire.* MR. FOWLER *comes in, and goes over to the writing desk.*)

MR. FOWLER

Ah, there you are, Miss Cooper. I've come for some note paper.

MISS COOPER

Any luck, Mr. Fowler?

MR. FOWLER

I'm afraid not. I shall try again, of course. I'm quite sure there's been some mistake—a telegram wrongly addressed, or something.

MISS COOPER

I expect so.

MR. FOWLER

I don't want anyone to wait up, but as I can hear the front door bell from my room, I wonder if you'd mind if I answer it myself tonight?

MISS COOPER

That's quite all right, Mr. Fowler, but you're surely not still expecting him, are you?

MR. FOWLER

He might have hired a car, you know. He's a very extravagant boy. You know what these artists are. Well, good night.

47

MISS COOPER

Good night, Mr. Fowler. (MR. FOWLER *goes out.* MISS COOPER *wanders over to inspect the muddy footprints on the carpet. She is on her knees as* JOHN *comes back. He sits down moodily, in silence.* MISS COOPER *methodically finishes scraping up pieces of dried mud, walks to the wastepaper basket and throws them in. Then she goes to* MRS. RAILTON-BELL's *unwanted coffee and pours a cup, black, with two lumps of sugar. Silently she hands it to him. He takes it, looking up at her, and sips it. She sits on the arm of his chair and leans her head affectionately on his shoulder. Gently*) Are you very drunk?

JOHN

No.

MISS COOPER

How many?

JOHN

As many as I could afford. It wasn't a lot.
   (*Pause. She takes his hand.*)

MISS COOPER

Something's the matter, isn't it?

JOHN

Nothing much.

MISS COOPER

Want to tell me?

JOHN

I can't tell you.

48

MISS COOPER
(*Cheerfully*)

That's all right. What did you say to the old women?

JOHN

Too much. Far too damn much. Oh, God! (*He puts the coffee down, gets up and walks away from her. She watches him anxiously*) I may have to leave.

MISS COOPER
(*Sharply*)

You can't leave.

JOHN

I may have to.

MISS COOPER

You won't have to. I'll see to that. But was it so bad?

JOHN
(*Bitterly*)

Not very bad, I suppose. Just an ordinary show-off, a rather sordid little piece of alcoholic self-assertion. Taking it out on two old women, telling them what a brilliant political thinker I am, hinting at what a great man I once was. I even gave away that I used to work in the docks.

MISS COOPER

Oh, Lord!

JOHN

And that I knew Roger Williamson. I think I covered that up, though. I hope I did.

49

MISS COOPER

I hope you did too, otherwise old Railton-Bell will be on to it like a bloodhound. Anything else?

JOHN

I don't know. I can't think now. I'll remember it all in the morning. (*Miserably*) Oh, Pat. I'm so sorry.
(*He puts his arm round her affectionately.*)

MISS COOPER

That's all right. I'll cover up for you. Finish your coffee.
(*He obediently takes the cup up again.*)

JOHN

Why do I do these things? I used to know how to behave.

MISS COOPER

(*Kissing him gently on the cheek*)
I'd do them too, in your place.

JOHN

Don't overdramatize me. I do that enough myself. I'd probably have been nothing.

MISS COOPER

What about that newspaper cutting about yourself you showed me. which prophesied—?

JOHN

One political tipster napping an outsider. If nothing happens his tip is forgotten. If, by a fluke, it does, he can say, "Look how clever I was twenty years ago—"

MISS COOPER

But before you were even thirty you'd been made a Junior Minister

JOHN

(Brusquely rising)

Yes, yes, yes. It doesn't matter. The world is full of promising young men who haven't, in middle age, fulfilled their promise. There's nothing to that. Nothing at all.

(He has turned away from her and is staring at the floor.)

MISS COOPER

(Quietly)

I wish you'd tell me what's happened.

JOHN

I can't. I've told you I can't. But it's not important.

MISS COOPER

Important enough for quite a few whiskies.

JOHN

A lot of things are important enough for that. The day I heard Willy Barker had been made a Cabinet Minister I had a bottle.

(Pause.)

MISS COOPER

Couldn't you *ever* get back?

(John laughs sharply.)

JOHN

God, what a field day for the Tory press that would be! John Malcolm Ramsden has decided to stand as a Labour Independent for his old constituency. It will be recalled that Mr. Ramsden, who was a Junior Minister in the 1945 Administration, went to prison for six months in 1946 on the triple charge of assaulting a police officer in the course of his duty, of being drunk and disorderly and of causing grievous bodily harm to his wife. The headline—Jailbird Stands Again. No, thank you. I'll stay John Malcolm—journalist, middle-aged soak and has-been, the terror of the older lady residents of the Hotel Beauregard, Bournemouth. That's vastly preferable, I assure you.

(*He has turned away from her again. She goes up to him quietly and puts her arms on his shoulders.*)

MISS COOPER

John, dear, I don't want to know what it is, but let me help you, if I can.

(*He turns round and gazes at her.*)

JOHN
(*Simply*)

Do you know, Pat, that I love you very sincerely?

MISS COOPER
(*With a smile*)

Sincerely? That sounds a little like what a brother says to a sister.

JOHN
(*With an answering smile*)

You have surely reason enough to know that my feelings for you can transcend the fraternal.

MISS COOPER

Yes. But for all that—and don't think I'm not grateful for all that —not really quite enough reason. (*They are drawing together when*

52

there is a sound outside the hall door and they move apart, not in alarm,
and as if from long practice. ANNE *comes in.* MISS COOPER *says*
brightly) Oh, hullo, Mrs. Shankland. They told me you'd gone up some
time ago.

ANNE

I had, but not to bed. I was reading.

MISS COOPER

That's a comfy armchair, in there, isn't it?

ANNE

Very.
 (*She stands, uncertainly, just inside the door, looking at* JOHN,
who, after a brief glance, has turned slightly away from her.)

MISS COOPER

Was there anything you wanted, Mrs. Shankland?

ANNE

(*Diffidently*)
No. I just wanted a word or two with—Mr. Malcolm.

MISS COOPER

(*Brightly again*)
Oh, really? Had you two met before?

ANNE

Yes. A long time ago.

53

MISS COOPER

Oh. (*She glances at* JOHN, *evidently disturbed at the danger to his anonymity inherent in this situation, but she gets no answering look*) Oh, well. I'll leave you two alone, then. If you want anything, I shall be up for quite a time yet.

(*She goes out, closing the door.* ANNE *gazes steadily at her ex-husband, but he is still looking away from her.*)

ANNE

I didn't want to go away without our saying something to each other, John. I hope you don't mind?

JOHN

Mind? Why should I mind?

ANNE

Your rushing out of dinner like a whirlwind made it look as if you hated the very sight of me.

JOHN

(*Slowly, looking at her fully for the first time*)
The very sight of you, Anne, is perhaps the one thing about you that I don't hate.

ANNE

(*With a slight, nervous laugh*)
Oh, dear. That's not very nice to hear.

JOHN

Don't you enjoy being complimented on your looks any more? Has your narcissism vanished?

ANNE

No. I suppose not. But I don't enjoy being hated by you.

JOHN

Don't you? You used to.

ANNE

You've got me wrong, John. You always did, you know.

JOHN

(*Quietly*)

I don't think so, Anne. If I had, I wouldn't have found you so predictable.

ANNE

You always used to say I was predictable. I remember that was one of the things that used to irritate me most. It's such an easy thing to say, and so impossible to disprove.

JOHN

Yes, yes, yes. I've no doubt. Go to bed, Anne, and disappear quietly tomorrow. It's better, really it is.

ANNE

No, John. Let me stay just a little longer. May I sit down?

JOHN

Is that a way of reminding me of my bad manners? I know I shouldn't sit while you're standing—

ANNE

(*Laughing gently*)

You're so bristly. Even bristlier now than before. (*She sits down*) Your manners were always very good.

JOHN

You used to tick me off about them often enough.

ANNE

Well—only sometimes—when we had silly conventional people at the flat who didn't understand you as I did.

JOHN

(*With a faint smile*)

I think if I'd been given time, I could have predicted that answer.

ANNE

(*With an answering smile*)

Oh, dear! Tell me, did you always find me so predictable—even at the very beginning?

JOHN

Yes.

ANNE

Why did you marry me, then?

JOHN

If it pleases your vanity to hear my answer once again, you shall. Because my love for you at that time was so desperate, my craving for you was so violent, that I could refuse you nothing that you asked—not even a marriage that every prompting of reason told me must be disastrous.

ANNE

Why did it so necessarily have to be disastrous?

JOHN

Because of class, mainly.

ANNE

Class? Oh, that's nonsense, John. It's just inverted snobbery.

JOHN

No. I don't think so. The gulf between Kensington Gore and the Hull Docks is still fairly wide. I was one of a family of eight, as I must have told you many a time, and my views of a wife's duties must have been at least a little colored by watching my mother sacrifice her health, strength and comfort and eventually her life to looking after us children, and to keeping the old man out of trouble. I'm not saying my demands on a wife would have been pitched as high as that. But they would, I think, at least have included the proper running of a home and the begetting of children.

ANNE

(*Hotly*)

About children, I did make it perfectly clear before our marriage—

JOHN

Yes. You made it perfectly clear. A famous model mustn't gamble her figure merely for posterity. I accepted the bargain, Anne, the whole bargain. I have no complaint.

ANNE

(*Angrily*)

You have, John. You know you have. Your real complaint is still the same as it always was—that I didn't love you when we got married—

JOHN

Oh, God! Do we have to go into that again?

ANNE

Yes, we do, it needs clearing up. You admitted just now that I was the one who wanted the marriage. All right. If that's true—which it is —what could have been the motive, except love? Oh, yes. I know. You were an undersecretary at the time, but, let's face it, there were even grander figures that I might have—

JOHN

(*Interrupting*)

I know, Ann dear. I remember it all in detail. A baronet, an Australian millionaire, and that film producer.

ANNE

Well, then?

JOHN

(*Quietly*)

You married me because you were frightened. You were going to be thirty. You'd realized suddenly that you couldn't go on for the rest of your life gazing joyously at yourself in the mirror, because the time would come when what you saw in the mirror would no longer give you joy. And you couldn't go on treading happily on the faces of all the men who wanted you, because the time would come when there wouldn't be so many faces to tread on.

ANNE

Eloquent, John, but unconvincing. If so, why not a baronet, or a millionaire? Why Mrs. Ramsden?

JOHN

Because the others couldn't pay you the full price.

ANNE

What price?

JOHN

The price you so reluctantly put on yourself when you settled for giving yourself to the highest bidder in marriage.

ANNE

You mean, a title wasn't enough?

JOHN

No.

ANNE

Nor a million?

JOHN

Nor a million.

ANNE

What was the price then?

JOHN

Enslavement.

ANNE

John, really. How ridiculous you are. I seem to remember this accusation from the old days—

JOHN

I've no doubt you do.

ANNE

If all I wanted to do was to make my husband a slave, why should I specially have chosen you and not the others?

JOHN

Because where would your fun have been in enslaving the sort of man who was already the slave of his own head gardener? You wanted bigger game. Wilder game. None of your tame baronets and Australian millionaires, too well-mannered to protest when you denied them their conjugal rights, and too well brought up not to take your headaches at bedtime as just headaches at bedtime. "Poor old girl! Bad show! So sorry. Better in the morning, I hope. Feeling a bit tired myself, anyway." No, Anne, dear. What enjoyment would there have been for you in using your weapons on that sort of a husband? But to turn them on a genuine, live, roaring savage from the slums of Hull, to make him grovel at the vague and distant promise of delights that were his anyway by right, or goad him to such a frenzy of drink and rage by a locked door that he'd kick it in and hit you with his fist so hard that you'd knock yourself unconscious against a wall—that must really have been fun.

ANNE
(*At length*)

Goodness, John, how you do go on.

JOHN

Yes. I do. You must forgive me. It's a foible, perhaps, of disappointed politicians. Besides, tonight I'm rather drunker than usual.

ANNE
(*With a hint of eagerness*)

Because of seeing me?

JOHN

Yes.

ANNE

I'm sorry.

JOHN

No you're not.

(ANNE *laughs, quite gaily now, and with far more confidence.*)

ANNE

You haven't changed much, have you?

JOHN

Haven't I?

ANNE

The same old John pouring out the same old cascade of truths, half-truths and distortions, all beaten up together, to make a neat, consistent story. *Your* story. Human nature isn't quite as simple as you make it, John. You've left out the most important fact of all.

JOHN

What's that?

ANNE

That you're the onl person in the world I've ever been really fond of. You notice how tactfully I leave out the word love. Give me a cigarette. (*He pulls a packet from his pocket*) Oh, not *still* those awful cork-tipped things. I'll have one of my own. Hand me my bag. (*A faint note of authority has crept back into her voice.* JOHN *obediently hands her her bag and she takes out a gold cigarette case*) Do you dispute that?

JOHN

I might observe that your fondness for me was sometimes shown in rather surprising ways—

ANNE

Well, I wasn't prepared to be your door mat. I had to fight back sometimes, didn't I?

JOHN

I suppose so. It was your choice of weapons that was unfair.

ANNE

I didn't have any others. You had the brains and the eloquence and the ability to make me feel cheap—which, incidentally, you've done again tonight.

JOHN

Have I? I'm sorry.

ANNE

Anyway, isn't it a principle of war that you always play on the opponent's weakness?

JOHN

A principle of war, not necessarily of marriage.

ANNE

Marriage is a kind of war.

JOHN

It is for you.

ANNE

(*With a smile*)

For you too, John. Be fair now.

JOHN

And the weakness you played on was my overpowering love for you?

ANNE

You can put it that way, if you like. There are less pretty-sounding ways. (JOHN *remains silent, looking at her as she smokes her cigarette, through a holder—now plainly quite confident of herself*) Besides, you and I never could have agreed on *that* aspect of married life.

JOHN

No. We couldn't.

ANNE

Why are you staring at me?

JOHN

You know very well why.

ANNE
(Contentedly)

Well, don't. It makes me embarrassed.

JOHN

I'm sorry.

ANNE

You really think I haven't changed much—to look at, I mean?

JOHN
(Not looking at her)

Not at all.

ANNE

Just a clever make-up, I expect.

JOHN

I don't think so.

63

ANNE

If you'd wanted an obedient little *hausfrau,* why didn't you marry one—like that manageress I caught you canoodling with a moment ago? That *was* a canoodle, wasn't it?

JOHN

A canoodle is what you would call it—yes.

ANNE

Why haven't you married her?

JOHN

Because I'm not in love with her.

ANNE

Does that matter?

JOHN

I'm old-fashioned enough to think it does.

ANNE

Couldn't you—as they say—*learn* to love her? After all, she's your type.

JOHN

I have still only one type in the whole world, Anne. God knows it does little for my pride to have to admit that to you, but I never was very good at lying about myself. (*Looking at her again*) Only one type. The pro-totype.

ANNE

(*Quietly*)

I'm glad.

64

JOHN

I've no doubt you are. Tell me, does a compliment still give you that little jab in the solar plexus that you used to describe to me?

ANNE

Yes, it does. More so than ever, now that I'm forty. There—I've admitted it.

JOHN

I'd worked it out anyway. (*They both laugh quietly. He picks up her cigarette case*) That's a nice little affair. Who gave you that? Your second?

ANNE

Yes.

JOHN

He had good taste.

ANNE

In jewels.

JOHN

You ought to have made a go of it with that man. He sounds much more your form.

ANNE

He wasn't a man. He was a mouse.

JOHN

Didn't he pay you enough compliments?

65

ANNE

Too many and none of them meant.

JOHN

No solar plexus?

ANNE

No. (*She takes his hand suddenly in an intimate friendly gesture*)
John, I'm in a bad way you know.

JOHN

I'm sorry.

ANNE

Some of the things you used to tell me might happen to me *are* happening.

JOHN

Such as?

ANNE

Loneliness—for one.

JOHN

No friends?

ANNE

Not many. I haven't the gift.

JOHN

There's no gift. To make people love you is a gift, and you have it—

ANNE
(*Bitterly*)

Had it—

JOHN

Have it.

ANNE

Yet I hate being alone. Oh, God, how I hate it. This place, for instance, gives me the creeps.

JOHN
(*Innocently*)

Why did you come here, then?

(*For the briefest instant she looks startled, but recovers at once.*)

ANNE

I suppose I didn't realize what it would be like. Oh, God! What a life. I can just see myself in a few years' time at one of those separate tables—

JOHN

Is there no one on the horizon?

ANNE

No one that I'd want. And time is slipping. God, it goes fast, doesn't it?

JOHN

I haven't found it to, these last eight years.

ANNE

Poor John. I'm so sorry. (*She squeezes his hand*) But it's such a wonderful fluke, our meeting again like this, that we really shouldn't waste it. We must see some more of each other now. After all, when fate plays as astounding a trick as this on us, it must mean something, mustn't it? Don't send me away tomorrow. Let me stay on a little while. (JOHN *makes no reply. He is staring at her. She continues speaking, gently*) I won't be a nuisance. (JOHN *still does not answer. He is still staring at her*) I won't, John. Really I won't.

JOHN
(*At length, murmuring thickly*)
You won't be a nuisance. (*He embraces her suddenly and violently. She responds. After a moment she begins to say something. He interrupts her, savagely*) Don't speak. For God's sake, don't speak. You'll kill this moment.

ANNE
Darling John, even at the risk of "killing your moment" I think I really *must* say something. I think I must remind you that we are in a public lounge, and inform you that Miss Cooper has been good enough to give me what appears to be a very isolated room, the number of which is—(*She pulls a key from her pocket*)—nineteen. Give me one of those horrid cork-tipped things of yours. I'm right out of mine. (*He takes a packet and brusquely thrusts them at her. She takes a cigarette. He tenders a lighter to her. His hand is trembling*) Oh—what a shaky hand! (*She holds it still and lights her cigarette.* JOHN *thrusts his hand back into his coat pocket and keeps it there. She gets up, gathers her bag in silence, smooths her dress, makes some adjustment to her hair, and turns to him*) How do I look? All right?

JOHN
(*Murmuring*)
All right.

68

ANNE
(Happily blowing him a kiss)

Darling John.

JOHN
(Not returning the gesture)

Darling Anne.

ANNE

Half an hour? *(She goes towards the door. Before she gets there,* MISS COOPER *can be heard calling* "Mrs. Shankland," *from the hall.* ANNE *stops and smiles at* JOHN) You see?
(The door opens and MISS COOPER *comes in.)*

MISS COOPER

Oh, Mrs. Shankland—you're wanted on the telephone—a London call.

ANNE

Oh? Where is the telephone?

MISS COOPER

I'll show you. It's just through here. *(The two women go out. Left alone,* JOHN *sits down suddenly, as if his knees had weakened. He rests his head on his hands. He is in that attitude when* MISS COOPER *comes back. She looks at him for a moment before she speaks)* That's her, isn't it?

JOHN

What?

MISS COOPER

Mrs. Shankland. That's the one, isn't it?

69

JOHN

Yes.

MISS COOPER

She looks exactly the way you described her. Carved in ice, you said once, I remember.

JOHN

Did I?

MISS COOPER

What's going to happen now John? (*He looks up at her without replying. There is a pause before she speaks again, quietly, at length*) I see. Well—I always knew you were still in love with her and always would be. You never made any bones about that—

JOHN
(*Pleadingly*)

Pat, dearest—

MISS COOPER

No. You don't need to say anything. I understand. So you'll be going away, will you?

JOHN

I don't know. Oh, God, I don't know.

MISS COOPER

I expect you will. She looks as if she'd got some will power, that girl. If she's taken that much trouble to run you to earth down here, she won't let you go so easily—

JOHN

She hasn't run me to earth. It was a coincidence, her coming down here.

MISS COOPER

Coincidence? Do you really believe that?

JOHN

Yes.

MISS COOPER

All right, then. I'm not saying anything.

JOHN

Say it.

MISS COOPER

No, I won't.
(*He jumps up and fiercely grabs her by the arms.*)

JOHN
(*Fiercely*)

Say it. Say it, damn you.

MISS COOPER
(*Quietly*)

Don't knock *me* about, John. I'm not her, you know.
(*He relaxes his grip.*)

MISS COOPER

All right. I'll say it. If it was coincidence, why is she talking to the editor of the *New Outlook* on the telephone now?

JOHN

What?

MISS COOPER

His name's Wilder, isn't it?

JOHN

Yes.

MISS COOPER

Terminus number?

JOHN

Yes.

MISS COOPER

And he knows who you really are, doesn't he, and where you live?

JOHN

Yes.

MISS COOPER

And he goes around the West End quite a bit, I'd imagine—cocktail parties and things? (JOHN *has sat down again, this time without replying*) Mind you it could be a different Mr. Wilder, I suppose. If there's one coincidence—why not another?

(ANNE *comes back. She looks happy and unruffled.*)

ANNE

(*To* MISS COOPER)

Thank you so much, Miss Cooper. I'm going to bed now. I've put down a call for 8.30 with hot water and lemon. I hope that's all right?

MISS COOPER

Quite all right, Mrs. Shankland.

ANNE

Well, good night. Good night, Mr. Malcolm.
(JOHN *gets up suddenly from his chair.*)

JOHN

Stay here, Anne. Pat, you go.

MISS COOPER
(*Urgently*)
Not now, John. Leave it till the morning.

JOHN

It's got to be now. (*He holds the door open for her*) Leave us alone,
Pat, please. (MISS COOPER *goes out quietly.* JOHN *closes the door after
her and turns to face* ANNE) When fate plays as astounding a trick as
this, it must mean something, Anne, mustn't it?

ANNE

Yes, that's what I said.

JOHN
(*Harshly*)
What did you tell Wilder? (ANNE *opens her mouth to speak*) No,
no. There's no need to lie any more. I'll quote you, shall I? My dear,
our little plot's gone off quite wonderfully. Thank you so much for
your help. Ten minutes alone with him was all I needed to have him
groveling. My dear, it was too funny, but after only one kiss his hand
was shaking so much he couldn't even light my cigarette. You should
have seen it. You'd have died laughing. Oh, yes. He's at my feet again,
all right, and I can tread on his face just any time I like from now on.
(*He has advanced on her slowly and stands facing her. She
stands her ground, but looks a little scared.*)

73

ANNE

(*Sincerely*)

John, please, don't be so angry with me. It's not as if I'd done anything so terrible. I had to see you again. I was desperate to see you
again, and this was the only way I could think of—

JOHN

The only way *you* could think of, of course. You wouldn't have
thought of writing me a letter, or ringing me up, or telling me the truth
in there? (*He points to the dining room*) Oh, no. You had to have
your conquest, you had to have your unconditional surrender, and if you
could do it by lying and cheating, so much the better. It makes the
greater triumph.

ANNE

That's not true. Really it isn't. Oh, yes, I should have told you, John.
Of course I should have told you, but, you see, even now I've still got
a little pride left—

JOHN

And so have I, Anne, thank God. So have I. (*He puts his hands on her
arms and pulls her close to him, staring at her face*) Yes, I can see the
make-up now all right. Yes, Anne, I can see little lines there that weren't
there before and it won't be very long now before this face will begin to
decay and then there'll be nothing left to drive a man to—
(*He has slipped his hands on to her throat*)

ANNE

(*Quietly*)

Why don't you?
(*He stands looking down at her for a moment and then pushes
her violently away. She falls from the chair on which she
has been sitting, and in her fall knocks over an occasional table.*

74

JOHN *goes to the French windows, pulls them open, and runs out. The wind blows the curtains into the room. She gets up from the floor and stands quite still, her face expressionless. There is a mirror over the fireplace and she stares at herself for a long time. She turns quickly away and begins to sob, quietly at first, and then more violently, until, as she makes her way blindly to the hall door, it is uncontrollable.* MISS COOPER *comes in before* ANNE *has reached the door.* ANNE, *seeing her barring the way, runs back into the room, still sobbing.* MISS COOPER *deliberately closes the windows, before turning to* ANNE. *Then she approaches her and puts her hand on her shoulder.*)

MISS COOPER

Come to my room, won't you, Mrs. Shankland? There's a fire there and a nice comfortable chair and I've even got a little sherry, I think. We'll be quite cosy there and no one can disturb us. (*She begins to move her towards the door*) You see, someone might come in here, and we don't want that, do we? Come along now, Mrs. Shankland. Come along—

(*She is leading her towards the door as*

The Lights Fade

Scene III

The dining room, the following morning. MISS MEACHAM *sits at her table, poring over the sporting page of a morning paper. The two undergraduates are at their table reading. The other tables have been occupied, except for the table by the window, and* ANNE'S. MISS COOPER *comes in from the lounge.*

MISS COOPER

(*Talking into the lounge*)
Yes, Mrs. Railton-Bell, I promise I will. (*The murmur of* MRS. RAILTON-BELL'S *voice can be heard off*) Yes, utterly disgraceful, I quite agree. I shall speak to him most severely. (*She closes the door with a faint sigh. Then, brightly, to the two undergraduates*) Good morning, Miss Tanner. Good morning, Mr. Stratton. (*They reply with a polite murmur and plunge back into their books*) Good morning, Miss Meacham. It looks as if we're going to have a nice dry day at last.

MISS MEACHAM

Is it going to be dry at Newbury?—that's the point. Walled Garden's a dog on heavy going.

MISS COOPER

Ah, now there you have me, Miss Meacham.
(MABEL *comes in.*)

MABEL

Miss Cooper, Mr. Malcolm wasn't in his room when I took his tea up, and his bed hadn't been slept in.

76

MISS COOPER

(*With a reassuring smile*)

Yes I know, Mabel.

MABEL

You know?

MISS COOPER

I should have told you, of course, but I'm afraid I clean forgot. He had to go to London unexpectedly last night.

MABEL

He won't be in to breakfast, then?

MISS COOPER

I don't suppose so.

(*The undergraduates go into the lounge.*)

MABEL

That's something anyway. It's nearly ten, now. What about the new lady? She's not down yet.

MISS COOPER

Yes, she's down, Mabel, but I don't think she's having breakfast.

MABEL

Not having breakfast?

MISS COOPER

She has to be very careful of her figure, you see.

MABEL

(*With puzzled gloom*)

Can't see what good a figure's going to be to you, when you're dead of starvation.

(*She goes into the kitchen.*)

MISS MEACHAM

She's leaving, isn't she, the new one?

MISS COOPER

Yes. She is. How did you know?

MISS MEACHAM

I heard her ask for her bags to be brought down. I knew she'd never stick it.

MISS COOPER

(*Coldly*)

Stick it, Miss Meacham?

MISS MEACHAM

Oh, I don't mean the hotel. Best for the price in Bournemouth. I've always said so. I meant the life. All this—(*She indicates the empty tables*)—She's not an "alone" type.

MISS COOPER

Is any type an "alone" type, Miss Meacham?

MISS MEACHAM

Oh, yes. They're rare, of course, but *you* are, for one, I'd say.

MISS COOPER

Am I?

MISS MEACHAM

Oh, I'm not saying you won't fall in love one day, and get married, or something silly like that. I'm only saying that if you don't, you'll be all right. You're self-sufficient.

MISS COOPER

(*A shade wearily, but polite*)

I'm glad you think so, Miss Meacham. Perhaps even a little gladder than you realize.

MISS MEACHAM

What do you mean by that?

MISS COOPER

I've no idea. I'm a bit tired this morning. I had very little sleep last night.

MISS MEACHAM

Well—I don't suppose you *are* glad, really. Probably you haven't had to face up to it yet. I faced up to it very early on—long before I was an old wreck—while I was still young and pretty and had money and position and could choose from quite a few. (*Reminiscently*) Quite a few. Well, I didn't choose any of them, and I've never regretted it—not for an instant. People have always scared me a bit, you see. They're so complicated. I suppose that's why I prefer the dead ones. Any trouble from them and you switch them off like a television set. (*She rises*) No, what I've always said is—being alone, that's the real blessed state —if you've the character for it. Not Mrs. What's-her-name from Mayfair, though. I could tell that at a glance. A couple of weeks here and she'd have her head in the gas oven. It's pork for lunch, isn't it?

MISS COOPER

Yes, Miss Meacham.

MISS MEACHAM

I loathe pork. Ah, well. I'd have a bit on Walled Garden, dear, if I were you. He's past the post if the going's on top.

(*She goes out.* MISS COOPER, *left alone, slumps wearily into the chair* MISS MEACHAM *has vacated. She washes out* MISS MEACHAM's *cup and pours some coffee out for herself. She sips it, and then lets her head fall wearily forward on to her chest, in an attitude of utter exhaustion. After a moment* JOHN *comes in slowly from the hall. After a look round he walks up to her quietly.*)

JOHN

(*In a low voice*)

Pet. I must see you a moment.

(MISS COOPER *opens her eyes and looks up at him. She jumps to her feet as she takes him in.*)

MISS COOPER

Are you all right?

JOHN

Yes, I'm all right.

MISS COOPER

Where did you go?

JOHN

I don't know. I walked a long way.

MISS COOPER

Were you out all night?

JOHN

No. I sat in a shelter for a time. Pat, I've got to have some money. I'm broke to the wide. I spent my whole week's check in the Feathers last night—

MISS COOPER

How much do you want?

JOHN

Enough to get me on a train and keep me some place for a few days. Three or four pounds, I suppose. Can you let me have it, Pat?

MISS COOPER

You won't need it, John. She's going.

JOHN

Are you sure?

MISS COOPER

Yes.

JOHN

Where is she now?

MISS COOPER

In my office. It's all right. She won't come in here. (*She feels his clothes*) Did you get very wet?

JOHN

Yes, I suppose so. It's dried off now.

MISS COOPER

You'd better sit down and have some breakfast. Your hands are like ice.

(*She rings a bell.*)

81

JOHN

I don't want anything to eat. Just some tea.

MISS COOPER

All right. Now sit down. Straighten your tie a bit, and turn your collar down. That's better. Now you look quite respectable.
(*She pulls out a chair for* JOHN *to sit down at his table.* DOREEN *comes in.*)

DOREEN

Yes, miss? (*Seeing* JOHN) Oh, you back? I suppose you think you can have breakfast at this time?

MISS COOPER

Just some tea, Doreen—that's all.

DOREEN

Okey doke.
(*She goes into the kitchen.*)

MISS COOPER

She'll have to go, that girl. (*She turns to* JOHN) Well, that was a fine way to behave, dashing out into the night, and scaring us out of our wits—

JOHN

Us?

MISS COOPER

Oh, yes. She was scared too. I stopped her from calling the police.

JOHN

So you talked, did you?

MISS COPPER

Most of the night. She was a bit hysterical and needed quieting. I didn't want to get a doctor.

JOHN

Did I—Pat, tell me the truth—did I hurt her?

MISS COOPER

Her throat? No.

JOHN

She fell though, didn't she? I seem to remember pushing her, and her falling and hitting her head—or perhaps I'm confusing it with—

MISS COOPER
(*Firmly*)

She's as right as rain. There isn't a mark on her of any kind.

JOHN
(*Murmuring*)

Thank God.
(DOREEN *comes in with a pot of tea and a plate.*)

DOREEN

I brought you some digestive biscuits. I know you like them.

JOHN

Thank you. Thank you, Doreen, very much.

DOREEN

Had a tumble or something? You've got mud all over your arm.

JOHN

What? Oh, yes. So I have. Yes, I remember now. I fell down last night in the dark.

DOREEN

Give it to me after and I'll get it off.
(*She goes out.*)

MISS COOPER

I should have seen that. I'm sorry.

JOHN

It's all right. They'll just think I was drunk. How is she this morning?

MISS COOPER

A bit shaky. Quieter, though. Did you know she took drugs?

JOHN

Drugs? What sort of drugs?

MISS COOPER

Oh, just those things that make you sleep. Only she takes about three times the proper dose and takes them in the day too.

JOHN

How long has this been going on?

MISS COOPER

About a year, I gather.

JOHN

The damn little fool. Why does she do it?

MISS COOPER

(*Shrugging*)

Why do you go to the Feathers? (*Pause*) Yes—there's not all that much to choose between you, I'd say. When you're together you slash each other to pieces, and when you're apart you slash yourselves to pieces. All told, it's quite a problem.

(*Pause.*)

JOHN

Why didn't she tell me about this last night?

MISS COOPER

Because she's what she is, that's why. If she'd shown you she was unhappy, she'd have had to show you how much she needed you, and that she'd never do—not her—not in a million years. Of course that's why she lied about coming down here. I've got rather a bad conscience about that, you know. I should never have told you. Just a flash of jealousy, I suppose. I'm sorry.

JOHN

What time is she leaving?

MISS COOPER

She's only waiting now to get some news of you. I was just going to start ringing up the hospitals. She asked me to do that.

JOHN

I see. Well, when I've finished this I'll slip out somewhere. You can tell her that I'm all right. Then when she's gone you can give me a ring.

MISS COOPER

You don't think you might tell her that yourself?

(*Pause.*)

JOHN

No.

MISS COOPER

It's your business, of course, but I think if I were in your place I'd want to.

JOHN

(*Savagely*)

You don't know what it's like to be in my place. You can't even guess.

MISS COOPER

(*Quietly*)

I think I can. Gosh, I'm tired. I shouldn't be sitting here gossiping with you. I've got work to do. You'd better let me tell her you're here.

JOHN

No, Pat, don't. Give me one good reason why I should ever see her again. Just one reason—

MISS COOPER

All right. Just one then. And God knows it's not for me to say it. Because you love her and because she needs your help.

(*Pause.*)

JOHN

(*Suspiciously*)

What went on between you two last night? How did she win you over?

MISS COOPER

She didn't win me over, for heaven's sake. Feeling the way I do, do you think she could? Anyway, to do her justice, she didn't even try. She didn't give me an act and I could see her as she is, all right. I think all you've ever told me about her is probably true. She *is* vain and spoiled and selfish and deceitful. Of course, with you being in love with her, you look at all those faults like in a kind of distorting mirror, so that they seem like monstrous sins and drive you to—well—the sort of thing that happened last night. Well, I just see them as ordinary human faults, that's all—the sort of faults a lot of people have—mostly women, I grant, but some men too. I don't like them but they don't stop me feeling sorry for a woman who's unhappy and desperate and ill and needing help more than anyone I have ever known. Well? Shall I call her in?

JOHN

No. Pat. No. Don't interfere in this. Just let her go back to London and her own life, and leave me to live the rest of mine in peace.

MISS COOPER
(*Quietly*)
That'd be fine, John, if you'd just tell me a little something first. Exactly what kind of peace *are* you living in down here?

JOHN

A kind of peace, anyway.

MISS COOPER

Is it? Is it even really living? (*He makes no reply*) Is it, John? Be honest, now. Oh, I know there's your work and your pals at the Feathers and—well—me—but is it even living?
(*Pause.*)

JOHN
(*Brusquely, at length*)
It'll do.

MISS COOPER

(*With a faint laugh*)

Thank you. I'm glad you didn't hand me one of those tactful tarra-diddles. I *did* try—you know—when we first began—you and I—all that time ago—I *did* try to help you to get back into some sort of life. As a matter of fact I tried very hard—

JOHN

I know you did.

MISS COOPER

It didn't take me long, though, to see I hadn't a hope.

JOHN

Don't blame me for that, Pat. Circumstances, as they say, outside my control—

MISS COOPER

Outside your control? Yes. That's right. (*Quite brightly*) When you think of it it seems really rather a pity you two ever met, doesn't it?

JOHN

Yes. A great pity.

MISS COOPER

(*Brightly*)

If you hadn't, she'd have been a millionairess, and you'd have been Prime Minister, and I'd have married Mr. Hopkins from the bank, and then we'd have all been happy. I'm going into my office now and I'm going to tell her you're here. I'll have a word with Mr. Fowler first, about a room he didn't take up, so if you want to skedaddle, you can. The door's through there and the street's outside, and down the street is the Feathers. It's a bit early, but I've no doubt they'll open for you. (*She goes into the lounge. As she goes:*) Oh, Mr. Fowler, I'm so sorry to bother you, but I just want to have a word—

> (*The door closes behind her. Left alone,* JOHN *stands in evident doubt and irresolution. Then he sits down at his table.* DOREEN *comes in.*)

DOREEN

Have you finished?

JOHN

Not quite, Doreen.

DOREEN

Make up your mind. (*She begins to clear some things from the other tables.* ANNE *comes in from the lounge.* JOHN *doesn't look at her*) Oh, hullo, Mrs. Shankland. You're a bit late for breakfast, I'm afraid. I expect you didn't know. There's some coffee left, though, or tea if you'd rather, and I can get you some biscuits. Is that all right?

ANNE

Thank you. That's very kind. Coffee please. Not tea.

DOREEN

Righty-oh.
> (*She goes into the kitchen.*)

ANNE
> (*Standing by* JOHN's *table, pleadingly*)

John. (*He doesn't look up*) John—

JOHN
(*Quietly*)

You'd better sit at your table. She'll be back in a moment.

ANNE

Yes. Yes, I will. (*She sits down at her table. He remains at his*) I was desperately worried about you.

JOHN

You needn't have been. I was quite all right. How are *you* now?

ANNE

All right too. (*After a pause*) I'm going this morning, you know.

JOHN

So I heard.

ANNE

I won't bother you again. Ever again. I just wanted to say I'm sorry I had to lie to you—

JOHN

Thank you, Anne.

ANNE

I don't know why I did. Not for the reasons you gave, I think, though they may be right too, I admit. I don't seem to know very much about myself any more. I'm sorry, John.

JOHN

That's all right.

ANNE

I *am* an awful liar. I always have been—ever since school. I don't know why but I'd rather lie than tell the truth even about the simplest things. (*With a wan smile*) It was nearly always about my lying that we used to quarrel in the old days—do you remember?

JOHN

Yes. I remember.

(ANNE *lowers her head quickly as the tears come suddenly.*)

ANNE

Oh, John. I don't know what's going to happen to me—

(DOREEN *comes in with a tray.* ANNE *turns her head quickly away from her.* DOREEN *goes to* JOHN's *table first, and puts down a plate of biscuits.*)

DOREEN

Thought you might like some more. I know your appetite. (*She goes to* ANNE's *table with some biscuits.* ANNE *has managed to wipe her eyes unseen*) Here you are, Mrs. Shankland.

ANNE

Thank you.

DOREEN

Coffee's just coming.

(DOREEN *goes out, having noticed nothing.*)

ANNE

(*Smiling again*)

Narrow escape. I'm sorry. I'm in a rather weak state this morning.

JOHN

How much money exactly does Shankland give you, Anne?

ANNE

I've told you—seven fifty. (*She meets his eyes. At length, murmuring shamefacedly*) Fifteen hundred.

JOHN

Can't you live quite happily on that?

ANNE

How can *I* live happily on anything now?

JOHN

But you don't need to be alone in London. You may not have many friends, but you have hundreds of acquaintances, and surely you can go out and enjoy yourself—

ANNE

You can be more alone in London than in this place, John. Here at least you can talk from table to table. In London it's the phone and usually no answer.
(*Pause.*)

JOHN

You must give up those drugs, Anne.

ANNE

She told you?

JOHN

They won't help, you know.

ANNE

I know they won't.

JOHN

Throw them all into the dust bin. They're no good, those things.

ANNE

I won't do that. I can't. I'm not strong enough. But I'll cut them down if I can.

JOHN

Try.

ANNE

I *will* try. I promise.
(*Pause.*)

JOHN

Tell me, Anne. When you say you need me, is it me you really mean, or just my love? Because if it's my love, you must know now that you have that. You have that for life.

ANNE

It's you, John.

JOHN

But why? Why, for heaven's sake?

ANNE

I suppose because you're all the things I'm not. You're honest and true and sincere and dependable and (*She breaks off and tries to smile*) —Oh, dear, this is just becoming a boring catalogue of your virtues. Too embarrassing. I'm sorry, and that damn waitress will come in and catch me crying again.

JOHN
(*Slowly*)

I may have had some of those virtues once, Anne. I'm not at all sure that I have them now, so I don't know if I'd be able to satisfy your need. I do know though that you can never satisfy mine.

ANNE

How can you know?

JOHN

Experience.

ANNE

Supposing I'd learnt something from the last eight years?

JOHN

It's not a lesson that can be learnt.

ANNE

I could still try.

JOHN

So could I, Ann. So could I. And we'd both fail.

ANNE

How can you be so sure?

JOHN

Because our two needs for each other are like two chemicals that are harmless by themselves, but when brought together in a test tube can make an explosive as deadly as dynamite.

ANNE

(*Shrugging*)

I could take the risk. After all, there are worse deaths, aren't there? (*She looks round the room at the empty tables*) Slower and more painful and more frightening. So frightening, John. So frightening. (*She lowers her head as once more the tears come*) I'm an awful coward, you see. I never have been able to face anything alone—the blitzes in the war, being ill, having operations, all that. And now I can't even face—just getting old.

(JOHN *gets up quietly from his table and walks to hers. She has her head lowered and a handkerchief to her eyes, so that it is only when she has recovered herself a little that she finds him sitting there. She looks at him without saying anything. He takes her hand.*)

JOHN
(*Gently*)

You realize, don't you, that we haven't very much hope together?
(ANNE *nods, and holds his hand tight in hers.*)

ANNE

Have we all that much apart?
(DOREEN *comes in with* ANNE's *coffee. They release their hands.*)

DOREEN
(*Seeing them*)

Oh. (*To* JOHN) Do you want your tea over there?

JOHN

Yes, please. (*She brings his cup over, and gives* ANNE *her coffee*) Thank you.

DOREEN

Do you two want to sit at the same table from now on? You can, if you like.

JOHN

Yes. I think we do.

DOREEN

Oh. I'll make up a double for you for lunch then. It's just so long as we know—

(She goes into the kitchen. JOHN *once again takes* ANNE's *hand.)*

Curtain

TABLE NUMBER SEVEN

A Play in Two Scenes

TABLE NUMBER SEVEN

(In Order of Speaking)

JEAN STRATTON	Ann Hillary
CHARLES STRATTON	Donald Harron
MAJOR POLLOCK	Eric Portman
MR. FOWLER	William Podmore
MISS COOPER	Beryl Measor
MRS. RAILTON-BELL	Phyllis Neilson-Terry
MISS RAILTON-BELL	Margaret Leighton
LADY MATHESON	Jane Eccles
MISS MEACHAM	May Hallatt
MABEL	Georgia Harvey
DOREEN	Helena Carroll

Time: Summer.

Scene 1—Lounge. After tea.

Scene 2—Dining Room. Dinner.

Scene I

The lounge of the Beauregard Private Hotel. It is, perhaps, eighteen months or so since the events of the preceding play, but apart from a rearrangement of the chairs to accord with the summer season, and a set of new covers on those chairs, there has been little alteration.

CHARLES STRATTON, *in flannels and sport shirt, lies on the sofa, reading some large medical treatise. Through the French windows, which are open,* JEAN STRATTON (*née* JEAN TANNER) *appears, pulling a pram.*

JEAN

(*To the unseen baby*)

Tum along now. Tum along. Tum and see Daddy—Daddy will give you a little tiss and then beddy-byes—

(CHARLES' *face shows his annoyance at the interruption to his studies.*)

CHARLES

Bedtime, already?

JEAN

After six. How are you getting along?

CHARLES

Miles behind. Endless interruptions. It was idiotic to come back to this place. I should have remembered what it was like from the last time. We could have borrowed David's cottage—

JEAN

Nasty air in the Thames Valley. Not good for baby. Bournemouth air much better (*To baby*) isn't it, my little lammykins? He says, Yes Mummy, lovely air, lovely sun, makes baby teep like an ickle top—

CHARLES

He doesn't say anything of the sort. All he ever appears to say is "goo." I'm getting a bit worried.

JEAN

Don't be silly, darling. What do you expect him to do at five months? Quote T. S. Eliot?

CHARLES

I think all this "tum along" stuff you smother him in is bad for him. It's very dangerous, too, you know. It can lead to arrested development later on—

JEAN
(*Complacently*)

What nonsense you do talk. (*She has now sat on the sofa beside him and kisses him fondly. He turns from the caress a trifle brusquely*) Give me a proper kiss.

CHARLES
(*Murmuring*)

A kiss, but not a tiss.
(*He kisses her with a little more warmth, then breaks off.*)

JEAN

Go on.

CHARLES

No.

JEAN

Why not?

CHARLES

It's too early.

JEAN

You're so horribly coarse-grained sometimes that I wonder why I love you so much. But I do, you know, that's the awful thing. I've been thinking all the afternoon how much I loved you. Funny how it seems sort of to have crept up on me like this— Did it creep up on you too, or did you lie in your teeth before we got married?

CHARLES

I lied in my teeth. Now take baby up to beddy-byes, dear, and leave Daddy to his worky-perky—or Daddy won't ever become a docky-wocky.
(*There is the sound of a loud jovial voice in the garden.*)

MAJOR POLLOCK
(*Off*)

Hullo, 'ullo, Miss Meacham. Working out the form, eh? Got any tips for tomorrow?

MISS MEACHAM
(*Off*)

Let me see.

CHARLES

Oh, God! Here's the Major. Go on, darling, for heaven's sake. If he sees the baby, we're lost. He'll talk for hours about infant welfare in Polynesia or something.

JEAN

All right. (*To baby*) Tum along then—(*She meets* CHARLES' *eyes.*

Firmly) Come along, then, Vincent Michael Charles. It is time for your bath and subsequently for your bed. Better?

MISS MEACHAM
(*Off*)

Red Robin in the three-thirty.

CHARLES

Much.
(*He blows her a kiss as she goes out into the hall with the pram, from which emerges a faint wail.*)

JEAN
(*As she goes*)

Oh. Did Mummy bring him out of 'ovely garden into nasty dark pace. Naughty Mummy.
(*Her voice subsides.* CHARLES *returns to his book.*)

MAJOR POLLOCK
(*Off*)

Red Robin in the three-thirty? I'll remember that. Not that I can afford much these days, you know. Not like the old days when one would ring up the hall porter at White's, and get him to put on a couple of ponies. Lovely day, what?

MISS MEACHAM
(*Off*)

Not bad.
(MAJOR POLLOCK *comes in. He is in the middle fifties, with a clipped military moustache and extremely neat clothes. In fact, both in dress and appearance he is almost too exact a replica of the retired major to be entirely true.*)

MAJOR POLLOCK

Hullo, Stratton. Still at it?

104

CHARLES

(*With only the most perfunctory look-up from his book*)
Yes, Major.

MAJOR POLLOCK

Don't know how you do it. Really don't. Most praiseworthy effort,
I think.

CHARLES

Thank you, Major.
(*Pause. The* MAJOR *sits.*)

MAJOR POLLOCK

Of course when I was at Sandhurst—oh, so sorry—musn't disturb
you, must I?

CHARLES

(*Politely lowering his book*)
That's all right, Major. When you were at Sandhurst?

MAJOR POLLOCK

Well, I was going to say that I was a bit like you. Off duty, while most
of the other young fellers were gallivanting about in town, I used to be
up in my room, or in the library there, cramming away like mad. Military history—great battles of the world—Clausewitz—that sort of stuff.
I could have told you quite a lot about Clausewitz once.

CHARLES

Oh. And you can't now?

MAJOR POLLOCK

No. Afraid not. Everything goes, you know. Everything goes. Still I
didn't regret all those hours of study at the time. I did jolly well at Sandhurst.

CHARLES

Did you get the Sword of Honour?

MAJOR POLLOCK

What? No. Came quite close to it, though. Passed out pretty high. Pretty high. Not that it did me much good later on—except that they made me battalion adjutant because I was good at paper work. Could have been brigade major, as it happens. Turned it down because I thought, if trouble came—well—you know—miles behind the line— away from one's own chaps. I suppose it was a bit foolish. I'd probably have been a general now, on full pay. Promotion was always a bit tight in the Black Watch. Should have chosen another regiment, I suppose.

CHARLES
(*Plainly hoping to terminate the conversation*)

Yes.

MAJOR POLLOCK

Go on, my boy. Go on. So sorry. I talk too much. That's usually the trouble with old retired majors, what.

CHARLES

Not at all, sir. But I *will* go on, if you don't mind. I've rather a lot to do. (*There is a pause.* CHARLES *continues reading. The* MAJOR *gets up and, taking infinite pains not to make a sound, tiptoes to a table where he picks up a magazine, and tiptoeing back, sits down again.* CHARLES *has plainly been aware of the* MAJOR'S *tactfully silent passage.* MR. FOWLER *comes through the French windows, holding a letter.*)

MR. FOWLER

Oh, hullo, Major. I've just had the most charming letter—

MAJOR POLLOCK

(*Putting his fingers to his lips, and indicating* CHARLES)

Sh! (CHARLES *gets up resignedly and goes to the door*) Oh, I say. I do hope we're not driving you away.

CHARLES

No, that's quite all right. I can always concentrate much better in my room.

MAJOR POLLOCK

But you've got the baby up there, haven't you?

CHARLES

Yes, but it's a very quiet baby. It hasn't learnt to talk yet.
(*He goes out.*)

MAJOR POLLOCK

Well, Fowler, who's your letter from? An old flame?

MR. FOWLER

(*Chuckling happily*)

Old flame? I haven't got any old flames. I leave that to you galloping majors.

MAJOR POLLOCK

Well, I used to do all right once, I must say. In the regiment they used to call me Bucko Pollock. Regency buck—you see. Still, those days are past and gone. *Eheu fugaces, Postume, Postume.*

MR. FOWLER

(*Correcting his accent*)

Eheu fugaces, Postume, Postume. Didn't they teach you the new pronunciation at Wellington?

MAJOR POLLOCK

No. The old.

MR. FOWLER

When were you there?

MAJOR POLLOCK

Now, let's think. It must have been nineteen eighteen I went up—

MR. FOWLER

But they were using the new pronunciation then, I know. Our head classics master was an old Wellingtonian, and I remember distinctly his telling me—

MAJOR POLLOCK

Well, perhaps they did and I've forgotten it. Never was much of a hand at Greek.

MR. FOWLER
(*Shocked*)

Latin. Horace.

MAJOR POLLOCK

Horace, of course. Stupid of me. (*Plainly changing the subject*) Well, who *is* your letter from?

MR. FOWLER

It's a boy who used to be in my house and I haven't heard from for well over ten years. Brilliant boy he was, and done very well since. I can't think how he knew I was down here. Very good of him, I must say.

MAJOR POLLOCK

What happened to that other ex-pupil of yours—the painter feller?

MR. FOWLER

Oh. I still read about him in the newspapers occasionally. But I'm afraid I don't get much personal news of him. We've—rather lost touch, lately.

(MISS COOPER *comes in with a newspaper under her arm.*)

MISS COOPER

Good afternoon, Major, we've managed to get your copy of the *West Hampshire Weekly News.*

MAJOR POLLOCK
(*Eagerly*)

Good afternoon, Miss Cooper.

MISS COOPER
(*Handing him the newspaper*)

Joe had to go to three places before he could find one.

MAJOR POLLOCK

Thank you very much.

MISS COOPER

What was the urgency?

MAJOR POLLOCK

Oh—I just wanted to have a look at it, you know. I've never read it —strange to say—although I've been here—what is it—four years?

MISS COOPER

I'm not surprised. There's never anything in it except parking offenses and cattle shows.

(*The* MAJOR *opens the paper, turning away from her.*)

MAJOR POLLOCK

Well, thanks anyway.

MR. FOWLER

I've had a charming letter, Miss Cooper, from someone I haven't seen or heard from in over ten years.

MISS COOPER

(*Brightly*)

How nice. I'm so glad.

MR. FOWLER

I'm going to write to him and ask him if he'd care to come down for a day or two. Of course he probably won't—but just in case he does, will that room be vacant?

MISS COOPER

Not at the moment, I'm afraid, Mr. Fowler. We have so many casuals. But at the end of September—

MR. FOWLER

Good. I'll ask him for then. (*During this interchange between* MISS COOPER *and* MR. FOWLER, MAJOR POLLOCK, *unseen by them, has turned the pages of his newspaper over quickly, as if searching for something. Suddenly his eye is evidently caught by what he reads, and he folds the paper back with a sharp sound.* MR. FOWLER *looks up at him*) You were with the Highland Division at Alamein, weren't you, Major?
(*There is no immediate reply. When the* MAJOR *does look up his eyes are glassy and staring.*)

MAJOR POLLOCK

What? No. No, I wasn't. Not with the Highland Division.

MR. FOWLER

I thought you were.

MAJOR POLLOCK
(*Almost fiercely*)

I never said so.

MR. FOWLER

I just wondered because this boy—Macleod his name is—James, I think, or John—anyway he was known at school as Curly—he says in this letter he was with the Highland Division. I just wondered if you'd run into him at all.

MAJOR POLLOCK

Macleod? No. No, I don't think so.

MR. FOWLER

Well, of course, it would have been very unlikely if you had. It was just possible, though. (*He goes to the door.* MISS COOPER *has been straightening cushions and tidying up.* MAJOR POLLOCK *sits down, holding his paper, and staring blankly into space.* MR. FOWLER *murmurs to himself*) Curly Macleod. He once elided a whole word in his Greek Iambics—

(*He chuckles to himself and goes out.* MAJOR POLLOCK *looks down again at his paper, and, as* MISS COOPER *straightens herself from her labors, pretends to be reading it casually.*)

MAJOR POLLOCK

Yes. Pretty dull, I grant you.

MISS COOPER

What?

MAJOR POLLOCK

This paper. I don't suppose it's much read, is it?

MISS COOPER

Only by locals, I suppose. Farmers, estate agents—those sort of people.

MAJOR POLLOCK

I've never heard of anyone in the hotel reading it—have you?

MISS COOPER

Oh, yes. Mrs. Railton-Bell takes it every week.

MAJOR POLLOCK

Does she? Whatever for?

MISS COOPER

I don't know, I'm sure. There's not a lot that goes on in the world—even in West Hampshire—that she likes to miss. And she can afford fourpence for the information, I suppose.

MAJOR POLLOCK
(*Laughing jovially*)
Yes, I suppose so. Funny, though—I've never seen her reading it.

MISS COOPER

Oh, she gets a lot of things sent in to her that she never reads. Most of the stuff on that table over there is hers—

MAJOR POLLOCK

Yes. Yes, I know. She'd have had hers this morning then, I suppose?

MISS COOPER

Yes. I suppose so.

MAJOR POLLOCK

Oh. Dash it all. Here I've gone and spent fourpence for nothing. I mean, I could have borrowed hers, couldn't I?

(*He laughs heartily.* MISS COOPER *smiles politely and, having finished her tidying up, goes to the door.*)

MISS COOPER

I know you don't like venison, Major, so I've ordered you a chop for lunch tomorrow. Only I must ask you to be discreet about it, if you don't mind.

MAJOR POLLOCK

Yes, of course. Of course. Thank you so much, Miss Cooper.

(MISS COOPER *goes out.* MAJOR POLLOCK *opens the paper quickly and stares at it for some time, reading avidly. Then he suddenly rips out the whole page, crumpling it up and thrusting it into his pocket. Then he goes quickly to the table, and, after a feverish search, finds the* West Hampshire Weekly News. *He has turned it over to find the evidently offending page when* MRS. RAILTON-BELL *walks into the room from the hall, followed by her daughter* SIBYL. *The latter is a timid-looking, wizened creature in her thirties, bespectacled, dowdy and without make-up.*)

MRS. RAILTON-BELL

(*As she enters*)

Well, if that's what you meant, you should have said so, dear. I wish you'd learn to express yourself a little bit better— Good afternoon, Major Pollock.

MAJOR POLLOCK

Good afternoon, Mrs. Railton-Bell. (*Jovially to* SIBYL) Afternoon, Miss R.B. (*He is holding the paper, unable to hide it, or put it back on the table. He sees that* MRS. RAILTON-BELL *has noticed it*) I'm so sorry. I was just glancing through your *West Hampshire News.* I wonder if you'd let me borrow it for a few moments. There's something in it I want to see.

MRS. RAILTON-BELL

Very well, Major. Only please return it.

MAJOR POLLOCK

Of course.
(*He goes to the door.* MRS. RAILTON-BELL *has moved to her seat. As she does so she picks up the other copy of the* West Hampshire Weekly News *from the floor, where* MAJOR POLLOCK *has dropped it.*)

MRS. RAILTON-BELL

What's this? Here's another copy—

MAJOR POLLOCK

(*Feigning astonishment*)
Of the *West Hampshire Weekly News?*

MRS. RAILTON-BELL

Yes.

MAJOR POLLOCK

Well, I'm dashed.

MRS. RAILTON-BELL

It was on the floor over here.

MAJOR POLLOCK

Must be one of the casuals, I suppose.

MRS. RAILTON-BELL

You'd better take it, anyway, and leave me mine.

MAJOR POLLOCK

(*Doubtfully*)

You don't think, whoever owns it might—

MRS. RAILTON-BELL

If it's been thrown down on the floor, it's plainly been read. I'd like mine back, if you don't mind, please, Major.

MAJOR POLLOCK

(*Conceding defeat*)

Righty-oh. I'll put it back with the others. (*He does so, and takes the other copy from* MRS. RAILTON-BELL) Think I'll just go out for a little stroll.

SIBYL

(*Shyly*)

You don't happen to want company, do you, Major Pollock? I haven't had my walk yet.

MAJOR POLLOCK

(*Embarrassed*)

Well, Miss R.B.—jolly nice suggestion and all that—the only thing is I'm going to call on a friend—you see—and—

SIBYL

(*More embarrassed than he*)

Oh, yes, yes. Of course. I'm so sorry.

MAJOR POLLOCK

No, no. I'm the one who's sorry. Well, cheerie-bye till dinner.
(*He goes out.*)

MRS. RAILTON-BELL

I wish he wouldn't use that revolting expression. It's so common. But then he *is* common—

SIBYL

Oh, no, Mummy. Do you think so? He was in a very good regiment.

MRS. RAILTON-BELL

You can be in the Horse Guards and still be common, dear. (*Gently*) Sibyl, my dearest, do you mind awfully if your tactless old mother whispers something in your ear?

SIBYL

(*Resigned*)

No.

MRS. RAILTON-BELL

I didn't think it was *terribly* wise of you to lay yourself open to that snub just now.

SIBYL

It wasn't a snub, Mummy. I'm sure he really *was* going to see a friend— (MRS. RAILTON-BELL *smiles understandingly and sympathetically, shaking her head ever so slightly*) Well, I often *do* go for walks with the Major.

MRS. RAILTON-BELL

I know you do, dear. What is more, quite a lot of people have noticed it.

(*Pause.* SIBYL *stares at her mother.*)

SIBYL

(At length)

You don't mean—you can't mean— (*She jumps up and holds her cheeks with a sudden gesture*) Oh, no. How can people be so awful!

MRS. RAILTON-BELL

It's not being particularly awful when an unattached girl is noticed constantly seeking the company of an attractive older man.

SIBYL

(Still holding her cheeks)

They think I chase him. Is that it? They think I run after him, they think I want—they think—no, it *is* awful. It *is*. It *is*. It *is*.

MRS. RAILTON-BELL

(Sharply)

Quieten yourself, my dear. Don't get into one of your *states,* now.

SIBYL

It's all right, Mummy. I'm not in a state. It's just—well—it's just so dreadful that people should believe such a thing is even possible. I hate that side of life. I hate it.

MRS. RAILTON-BELL

(Soothingly)

I know you do, dear. But it exists, all the same, and one has to be very careful in this world not to give people the wrong impression. Quieter now?

SIBYL

Yes, Mummy.

MRS. RAILTON-BELL

Good. You must try not to let these things upset you so much, dear.

SIBYL

I only go for walks with the Major because I like hearing him talk. I like all his stories about London and the war and the regiment—and—well—he's seen so much of life and I haven't—

MRS. RAILTON-BELL

I don't know what you mean by that, dear, I'm sure.

SIBYL

I only meant— (*She checks herself*) I'm sorry.

MRS. RAILTON-BELL

(*Relentlessly pursuing her prey*)

Of course I realize that you must occasionally miss some of the gaieties of life—the balls and the cocktail parties and things—that a few other lucky young people can enjoy. I can assure you, dearest, if I could possibly afford it, you'd have them. But I *do* do my best, you know.

SIBYL

I know you do, Mummy.

MRS. RAILTON-BELL

There was Rome last year, and our Scandinavian cruise the year before—

SIBYL

I know, Mummy. I know. Don't think I'm not grateful. Please. It's only—
    (*She stops.*)

MRS. RAILTON-BELL

(*Gently prompting*)

Only what, dear?

SIBYL

If only I could *do* something. After all, I'm thirty-three—

MRS. RAILTON-BELL

Now, my dear. We've been over this so often. Dearest child, you'd never stand any job for more than a few weeks. Remember Jones & Jones?

SIBYL

But that was because I had to work in a basement, and I used to feel stifled and faint. But there must be something else.

MRS. RAILTON-BELL

(*Gently patting her hand*)

You're not a very strong child, dear. You must get that into your head. Your nervous system isn't nearly as sound as it should be.

SIBYL

You mean my *states*? But I haven't had one of those for a long time—

MRS. RAILTON-BELL

No, dear—you've been doing very well. Very well, indeed. But there's quite a big difference between not having hysterical fits and being strong enough to take on a job. (*Concluding the topic decisively*) Hand me that newspaper, would you, dear?

SIBYL

Which one?

119

MRS. RAILTON-BELL

The *West Hampshire Weekly News*. I want to see what the Major was so interested in. (SIBYL *hands her the paper*. MRS. RAILTON-BELL *fumbles in her pockets*) Oh, dear me, what a silly billy! I've gone and left my glasses and my book in the shelter at the end of Ragusa Road. Oh, dear, I do hope they're not stolen. I expect they're bound to be. Now—doesn't that show how dependent I am on you, my dear. If you hadn't had that headache you'd have been with me this afternoon, and then you'd never have allowed me to—

SIBYL

I'll go and look for them.

MRS. RAILTON-BELL

Oh, would you, dear? That really is so kind of you. I hate you to fetch and carry for me, as you know—but my old legs are just a wee bit tired— It was the far end of the shelter, facing the sea.

SIBYL

Where we usually sit? I know.
(She goes out. MRS. RAILTON-BELL *opens the paper and, scanning it very close to her eyes, she turns the pages to what she plainly knows, from past experience, to be the interesting section. Suddenly she stops moving the paper across her eyes. We do not see her face but the paper itself begins to shake slightly as she reads.* LADY MATHESON *comes in.*)

LADY MATHESON

Oh, hullo dear. It's nearly time for the newsreel.

MRS. RAILTON-BELL
(In a strained voice)
Gladys, have you got your glasses?

LADY MATHESON

Yes, I think so. (*She feels in her pocket*) Yes, here they are.

MRS. RAILTON-BELL

Then read this out to me.
(*She hands her the paper and points.*)

LADY MATHESON
(*Unsuspecting*)

Where, dear? Lorry driver loses license?

MRS. RAILTON-BELL

No, no. Ex-officer bound over.

LADY MATHESON
(*Brightly*)

Oh, yes. (*Reading*) "Ex-officer bound over. Offense in cinema."
(*Looking up*) In cinema? Oh, dear—do we really want to hear this?

MRS. RAILTON-BELL
(*Grimly*)

Yes, we do. Go on.

LADY MATHESON
(*Reading, resignedly*)

"On Thursday last, before the Bournemouth Magistrates, David An-
gus Pollock, fifty-five, giving his address as (*She starts violently*) the
Beauregard Hotel, Morgan Crescent—" (*In a feverish whisper*) Major
Pollock? Oh!

MRS. RAILTON-BELL

Go on.

LADY MATHESON

(*Reading*)

"Morgan Crescent—pleaded guilty to a charge of insulting behavior in a Bournemouth cinema." Oh! Oh! "On the complaint of a Mrs. Osborn, forty-three (*Breathlessly*) of 4 Studland Road." He must have been drinking—

MRS. RAILTON-BELL

He's a teetotaller.

LADY MATHESON

Perhaps just that one night.

MRS. RAILTON-BELL

No. Read on.

LADY MATHESON

"Mrs. Osborn, giving evidence, stated that Pollock, sitting next to her, persistently nudged her in the arm, and later attempted to take other liberties. She subsequently vacated her seat, and complained to an usherette. Inspector Franklin, giving evidence, said that in response to a telephone call from the cinema manager, Pollock had been kept under observation by police officers from three fifty-three P.M. until seven-ten P.M., by which time he had been observed to change his seat no less than five times, always choosing a seat next to a female person. There had, he admitted, been no further complaints, but that was not unusual in cases of this kind. On leaving the cinema Pollock was arrested and after being charged and cautioned stated: 'You have made a terrible mistake. You have the wrong man. I was only in the place half an hour. I am a colonel in the Scots Guards.' Later he made a statement. Appearing on behalf of the defendant, Mr. William Crowther, solicitor, stated that his client had had a momentary aberration. He was extremely sorry and ashamed of himself and would undertake never to behave in so stupid and improper a manner in future. He asked that his client's blameless record should be taken into account. He had enlisted in the army in 1925 and in 1939 was granted a commission as second lieutenant in the Royal Army Service Corps. During the war, he had held a responsible position in charge of an Army Supply Depot in the Orkney Islands, and had been discharged in 1946 with the rank of full lieutenant. Pollock was not called. The Chairman of the Bench, giving judgment, said: 'You have behaved disgustingly, but because this appears to be your first offense we propose to deal leniently with you.' The defendant was bound over for twelve months." (*She lowers the paper, disturbed and flustered to the core of her being*) Oh, dear. Oh, dear. Oh, dear.

MRS. RAILTON-BELL

(*Perfectly composed but excited*)

Thursday. It must have happened on Wednesday. Do you remember —he missed dinner that night?

LADY MATHESON

Did he? Yes, so he did. Oh, dear. It's all too frightful! I can hardly believe it. Persistently. It's so dreadful.

MRS. RAILTON-BELL

On the Thursday he was terribly nervous and depressed. I remember now. And then on the Friday, suddenly as bright as a button. Of course he must have read the papers and thought he'd got away with it. What a stroke of luck that I get this weekly one sent to me.

LADY MATHESON

Luck, dear? Is it luck?

MRS. RAILTON-BELL

Of course it's luck. Otherwise we'd never have known.

123

LADY MATHESON

Wouldn't that have been better?

MRS. RAILTON-BELL

Gladys! What *are* you saying?

LADY MATHESON

I don't know. Oh, dear. I'm so fussed and confused. No, of course, it wouldn't have been better. One has to know these things, I suppose— although sometimes I wonder why.

MRS. RAILTON-BELL

Because if there's a liar and a fraudulent crook and a—I can't bring myself to say it—wandering around among us unsuspected, there could be—well—there could be the most terrible repercussions.

LADY MATHESON

Well, he's been wandering around among us for four years now and there haven't been any repercussions yet. (*With a faint sigh*) I suppose we're too old.

MRS. RAILTON-BELL
(*Coldly*)

I have a daughter, you know.

LADY MATHESON

Oh. Poor Sibyl. Yes. And she's such a friend of his, isn't she? Oh, dear.

MRS. RAILTON-BELL

Exactly.

124

LADY MATHESON

(*After a moment's troubled reflection*)

Maud, dear—it's not my business, I know, and of course you have a mother's duty to protect your child—that, of course, I do see—and yet—well—she's such a strange girl—so excitable and shy—and so ungrown-up in so many ways—

MRS. RAILTON-BELL

Come to the point, Gladys.

LADY MATHESON

Yes, I will. It's this. I don't think you ought to tell her this.

MRS. RAILTON-BELL

Not *tell* her?

LADY MATHESON

Well, not all of it. Not the details. Say he's a fraud, if you like, but not—please, Maud—not about the cinema. (*Suddenly distressed by the thought herself*) Oh, dear! I don't know how I shall ever look him in the face again.

MRS. RAILTON-BELL

You won't have to, dear. (*She has risen purposefully from her chair*) I'm going to see Miss Cooper now, and insist that he leaves this hotel before dinner tonight.

LADY MATHESON

Oh, dear. I wonder if you should?

MRS. RAILTON-BELL

Gladys, what *has* come over you this evening? Of course I should.

LADY MATHESON

But you know what Miss Cooper is—so independent and stubborn sometimes. She might not agree.

MRS. RAILTON-BELL

Of course she'll agree. She *has* to agree if we all insist.

LADY MATHESON

But we don't *all*. I mean it's just the two of us. Shouldn't we consult the others first? (*Suddenly realizing the implication*) Oh, gracious! Of course that means we'll have to tell them all, doesn't it?

MRS. RAILTON-BELL
(*Delighted*)
An excellent idea, Gladys. Where's Mr. Fowler?

LADY MATHESON

In his room, I think.

MRS. RAILTON-BELL

And the young people? Shall we have them? They count as regulars by now, I suppose. Yes. We'll have them too.

LADY MATHESON

Oh, dear. I hate telling tales.

MRS. RAILTON-BELL

Telling tales? (*She points dramatically to the* West Hampshire Weekly News) The tale is told already, Gladys—to the world.

LADY MATHESON

Well, strictly speaking—only to West Hampshire.

MRS. RAILTON-BELL

Don't quibble, Gladys. (*At the French windows*) Miss Meacham's in the garden. I really don't think we need bother about Miss Meacham. She's so odd and unpredictable—and getting odder and more unpredictable every day. Here comes Sibyl. Go up and get the others down, dear. I'll deal with her.

LADY MATHESON

Maud, you won't— (SIBYL *comes in*) You'll remember what I said, won't you?

MRS. RAILTON-BELL

Yes, of course. Go on, dear. (LADY MATHESON *goes out*. MRS. RAILTON-BELL *turns to* SIBYL) Clever girl. You found them, did you, darling? (*She takes the book and the glasses from* SIBYL. *There is a pause. At length*) Sibyl dear. I think you'd better go to your room, if you don't mind.

SIBYL

Why, Mummy?

MRS. RAILTON-BELL

We're holding a meeting of the regulars down here to discuss a very urgent matter that has just cropped up.

SIBYL

Oh, but how exciting. Can't I stay? After all, I'm a regular, too—

MRS. RAILTON-BELL

I know, dear, but I doubt if the subject of the meeting is quite suitable for you.

SIBYL

Why, Mummy? What is it?

127

MRS. RAILTON-BELL

Oh, dear! You're such an inquisitive child. Very well, then. I'll tell you this much—but only this much. We are going to discuss whether or not we think that Miss Cooper should be told to ask Major Pollock to leave this hotel at once and never come back.

SIBYL

(*Aghast*)

What? But I don't understand. Why, Mummy? (MRS. RAILTON-BELL *does not reply*) Mummy, tell me, why?

MRS. RAILTON-BELL

I can't tell you, dear. It might upset you too much.

SIBYL

But I must know, Mummy. I must. What has he done?

MRS. RAILTON-BELL

(*After only the slightest hesitation*)

You really *insist* I should tell you?

SIBYL

Yes, I do.

MRS. RAILTON-BELL

Even after my strong warning?

SIBYL

Yes.

MRS. RAILTON-BELL

(*With a sigh*)

Very well, then, dear. I have no option, I suppose. (*With a quick ges-*

ture she hands the paper to SIBYL) Read that. Middle column. Half way
down. Ex-officer bound over.

(SIBYL *reads.* MRS. RAILTON-BELL *watches her. Suddenly* SIBYL *sits,
her eyes staring, but her face blank.* LADY MATHESON *comes in. She
sees* SIBYL *instantly.*)

LADY MATHESON
(*Shocked*)

Oh, Maud, you haven't—

MRS. RAILTON-BELL

I did my best, my dear, but she insisted. She absolutely insisted. (*Solici-
tously bending over her daughter's chair*) I'm so sorry, my dear. It must
be the most dreadful shock for you. It was for us too, as you can imagine.
Are you all right? (SIBYL *takes her spectacles off and folding the paper
meticulously, lays it down on the arm of her chair. She makes no reply.
Her mother tries again, slightly more sharply*) Are you all right, Sibyl?

SIBYL
(*Barely audible*)

Yes, Mummy.
(JEAN *comes in, looking rather annoyed.*)

JEAN

What is it, Mrs. Railton-Bell? I can only stay a moment. I must get
back to the baby.

MRS. RAILTON-BELL

I won't keep you long, I promise you. Take a seat. (*Turning to*
SIBYL, *sharply*) Sibyl, what have you done? (CHARLES *comes in. She
takes* SIBYL'S *glasses from her hand*) Look, you've broken your glasses.

SIBYL
(*Murmuring*)

How stupid.

CHARLES

Hullo, you've cut your hand, haven't you?

SIBYL

No.

CHARLES

Yes, you have. Let's see. (*With a rather professional air he picks up her limp hand and examines it*) Nothing much. No splinters. Here, you'd better have this. It's quite clean. (*He takes a clean handkerchief from his breast pocket and ties it neatly round her hand*) Iodine and a bit of plaster later.

(MR. FOWLER *has come in.*)

MRS. RAILTON-BELL

Ah, Mr. Fowler, good. Would you take a seat, and then we can begin. The two young people are in a hurry. I'm afraid I have very grave news for you all.

CHARLES

The boiler's gone wrong again?

MRS. RAILTON-BELL

No. I only wish it were something so trivial.

CHARLES

I don't consider shaving in cold, brown water trivial.

MRS. RAILTON-BELL

Please, Mr. Stratton.

MR. FOWLER
(*Anxiously*)

They're raising the prices again?

130

MRS. RAILTON-BELL

No. My news is graver even than that.

MR. FOWLER

I don't know what could be graver than that.

MRS. RAILTON-BELL

The news I have to give you, Mr. Fowler.

CHARLES

Look, Mrs. Railton-Bell, must we play twenty questions? Can't you just tell us what it is?

MRS. RAILTON-BELL
(*Angrily*)

My hesitation is only because the matter is so painful and so embarrassing for me that I find it difficult to choose my words. However, if you want it baldly, you shall have it. (*After a dramatic pause*) Major Pollock—who is not a major at all but a lieutenant promoted from the ranks in the R.A.S.C.—

CHARLES
(*Excitedly*)

No. You don't say! I knew it, you know. I always knew Sandhurst and the Black Watch was a phony. Didn't I say so, Jean?

JEAN

Yes, you did, but I said it first—that night he made the boob about serviettes.

MR. FOWLER
(*Chipping in quickly*)

I must admit I've always slightly suspected the public school education. I mean, only today he made the most shocking mistake in quoting Horace—quite appalling.

MRS. RAILTON-BELL

(*Raising her voice*)

Please, please, ladies and gentlemen. This is not the point. The dreadful, the really ghastly revelation is still to come. (*She gains silence, and once again pauses dramatically*) He was found guilty—

LADY MATHESON

Pleaded guilty—

MRS. RAILTON-BELL

Please, Gladys. He was found or pleaded guilty—I don't really see that it matters which—to behaving insultingly to no less than six respectable women in a Bournemouth cinema.

(*There is an aghast silence.*)

CHARLES

(*At length*)

Good God! What a performance.

LADY MATHESON

Really, Maud, I must correct that. I must. We only know one was respectable—the one who complained—and even she seemed a little odd in her behavior. Why didn't she just say straight out to the Major, "I do wish you'd stop doing whatever it is that you are doing"? That's what I'd have done. About the other five we don't know anything at all. We don't even know if he nudged them or anything.

MRS. RAILTON-BELL

Of course he nudged them. He was in that cinema for an immoral purpose—he admitted it. And he was seen to change his seat five times—always choosing one next to female persons.

CHARLES

That could make ten nudges, really, couldn't it? If he had the chance of using both elbows.

JEAN

Eleven, with the original one. Or twelve, supposing—

MRS. RAILTON-BELL

Really, we seem to be losing the essential point in a welter of trivialities. The point is surely that the Major—the so-called Major—has pleaded guilty to a criminal offense of a disgusting nature, and I want to know what action we regular residents propose to take.

MR. FOWLER

What action do you propose, Mrs. Railton-Bell?

MRS. RAILTON-BELL

I propose, on your behalf, to go to Miss Cooper and demand that he leaves the hotel forthwith.

CHARLES

No.

MRS. RAILTON-BELL

You disagree, Mr. Stratton?

CHARLES

Yes, I do. Please don't think I'm making light of this business, Mrs. Railton-Bell. To me what he's done, if he's done it, seems ugly and re-

133

pulsive. I've always had an intense dislike of the more furtive forms of sexual expression. So emotionally I'm entirely on your side. But logically I'm not.

MRS. RAILTON-BELL
(*Cuttingly*)

Are you making a speech, Mr. Stratton? If so, perhaps you'd like to stand over there and address us.

CHARLES

No. I'm all right where I am, thank you. I'm not making a speech either. I'm just saying that my dislike of the Major's offense is emotional and not logical. My lack of understanding of it is probably a shortcoming in me. The Major presumably understands my form of lovemaking. I *should* therefore understand his. But I don't. So I am plainly in a state of prejudice against him, and must be very wary of any moral judgments I may pass in this matter. It's only fair to approach it from the purely logical standpoint of practical Christian ethics, and ask myself the question: "What harm has the man done?" Well, apart from possibly slightly bruising the arm of a certain lady, whose motives in complaining—I agree with Lady Matheson—are extremely questionable—apart from that, and apart from telling us a few rather pathetic lies about his past life, which most of us do anyway from time to time, I really can't see he's done anything to justify us chucking him out into the street.

JEAN
(*Hotly*)

I don't agree at all. I feel disgusted at what he's done too, but *I* think I'm quite right to feel disgusted. I don't consider myself prejudiced at all, and I think that people who behave like that are a public menace and deserve anything they get.

CHARLES

Your vehemence is highly suspect. I must have you psychoanalyzed

JEAN

It's absolutely logical, Charles. Supposing next time it's a daughter—

CHARLES

(*Wearily*)

I know. I know. And supposing in twenty or thirty years' time she sits next to a Major Pollock in a cinema—

JEAN

Exactly. (*He laughs*) it's not funny, Charles. How would you feel—

CHARLES

Very ashamed of her if she didn't use her elbows back, very hard, and in the right place.

JEAN

Charles, I think that's an absolutely monstrous—

MRS. RAILTON-BELL

Please, please, please. This is not a private argument between the two of you. I take it, Mr. Stratton, you are against any action regarding this matter? (CHARLES *nods*) Of any kind at all? (CHARLES *shakes his head*) Not even a protest?

CHARLES

I might give him a reproving glance at dinner.

MRS. RAILTON-BELL

(*Turning from him in disgust*)

You, Mrs. Stratton, I gather, agree with me that I should see Miss Cooper?

JEAN
(*Firmly*)

Yes.

CHARLES
(*Murmuring to her*)

Book-burner.

JEAN
(*Furiously*)
What's book-burning got to do with it?

CHARLES

A lot.

MRS. RAILTON-BELL
(*Imperiously*)
Quiet, please. (*Turning to* MR. FOWLER) Mr. Fowler? What do you think?

MR. FOWLER
(*Confused*)
Well, it's difficult. Very difficult. I can't say I see it like Stratton. That's the modern viewpoint, I know—nothing is really wrong that doesn't do actual and assessable harm to another human being. But he's not correct when he calls that Christianity. Christianity, surely, goes much further than that. Certain acts are wrong because they are, in themselves and by themselves, impure and immoral, and it seems to me that this terrible wave of vice and sexual excess which seems to have flooded this country since the war might well, in part, be due to the decline of the old standards, emotional and illogical though they may well seem to the younger generation. Tolerance is not necessarily a good, you know. Tolerance of evil may itself be an evil. After all, it was Aristotle, wasn't it, who said—

(MISS MEACHAM *appears from the garden.*)

MISS MEACHAM

Oh, really—you've all gone on far too long about it. And when you start quoting Aristotle, well, personally, I'm going to my room.

MRS. RAILTON-BELL

You heard, Miss Meacham?

MISS MEACHAM

I couldn't help hearing. I didn't want to. I was doing my system and you need to concentrate like billy-oh on that, but I had my chair against the wall to catch the sun, and I wasn't going to move into the cold just for you people.

MRS. RAILTON-BELL

Well, as you know the facts, I suppose we should canvass your opinion. What is it?

MISS MEACHAM

I haven't any.

MRS. RAILTON-BELL

You must have *some* opinion?

MISS MEACHAM

Why should I? I've been out of the world for far longer than any of you and what do I know about morals and ethics? Only what I read in novels, and as I only read thrillers, that isn't worth much. In Mickey Spillane the hero does far worse things to his girls than the Major's done, and no one seems to mind.

MRS. RAILTON-BELL

I don't think that it's quite the point what Mickey Spillane's heroes do to his girls, Miss Meacham. We want your views on Major Pollock.

MISS MEACHAM

Do you? Well, my views on Major Pollock have always been that he's a crashing old bore, and a wicked old fraud. Now I hear he's a dirty old man, too, well, I'm not at all surprised, and quite between these four walls, I don't give a damn.

(*She goes out. There is a pause, and then* MRS. RAILTON-BELL *turns to* MR. FOWLER.)

MRS. RAILTON-BELL

Well, Mr. Fowler, I take it you are on the side of action?
(*Pause.*)

MR. FOWLER

I once had to recommend a boy for expulsion. Only once, in the whole of the fifteen years I was a housemaster. I was deeply unhappy about it. Deeply. And yet events proved me right. He was no good. He became a thief and a blackmailer, and—oh—horrible things happened to him. Horrible. (*After a moment's pause*) Poor boy. He *had* a way with him—

MRS. RAILTON-BELL

(*Impatiently*)
Are you in favor of action, Mr. Fowler?

MR. FOWLER

(*Unhappily*)
Yes, I suppose so. Yes, I am.

MRS. RAILTON-BELL

(*To* LADY MATHESON)
And you, Gladys? (*As* LADY MATHESON *hesitates*) You don't need to make a speech like the others, dear. Just say yes or no.
(*Pause.*)

LADY MATHESON
(*At length*)

Oh, dear!

MRS. RAILTON-BELL

Now, don't shilly-shally, Gladys. You know perfectly well what you feel about all this dreadful vice that's going on all over the country. You've told me often how people like that should be locked up—

LADY MATHESON
(*At length*)

Oh, dear!

MRS. RAILTON-BELL
(*Really impatient*)

Oh, for heaven's sake, make up your mind, Gladys. Are you on the side of Mr. Stratton with his defense of vice, or are you on the side of the Christian virtues like Mr. Fowler, Mrs. Stratton and myself?

CHARLES
(*Quietly*)

I have never in my life heard a question more disgracefully begged. Senator McCarthy could use your talents, Mrs. Railton-Bell.

MRS. RAILTON-BELL

Will you keep quiet! Well, Gladys, which is it to be?

LADY MATHESON

I'm on your side, of course. It's only—

MRS. RAILTON-BELL

(*To* CHARLES)

Well, Mr. Stratton—apart from Miss Meacham, who might be said to be neutral, the count appears now to be five to one against you.

CHARLES

Five to one?

MRS. RAILTON-BELL

My daughter, of course, agrees with me.

CHARLES

How do you know?

MRS. RAILTON-BELL

I know her feelings in this matter.

CHARLES

May we hear them from herself? (SIBYL, *during the whole of this discussion, has not stirred in her chair. Her two hands, one bound with a handkerchief, have rested motionless in her lap, and she has been staring at the wall opposite her*) Miss Railton-Bell—could we hear your views?
        (*There is no reply.*)

MRS. RAILTON-BELL

Mr. Stratton is asking you a question, dear.

SIBYL

Yes, Mummy?

CHARLES

Could we hear your views?

SIBYL

My views?

MRS. RAILTON-BELL

(*Clearly, as to a child*)

On Major Pollock, dear. What action should we take about him?
(SIBYL *seems puzzled and makes no reply. Her mother turns to the
others, in an aside*) It's the shock. (TO SIBYL *again*) You know what
you've just read in that paper, dear? What do you think of it?

SIBYL

(*In a whisper*)

It made me sick.

MRS. RAILTON-BELL

Of course it did, dear. That's how we all feel.

SIBYL

(*Her voice growing louder in a crescendo*)

It made me sick. It made me sick. It made me sick. It made me sick.

MRS. RAILTON-BELL

(*Going quickly to her and embracing her*)

Yes, dear. Yes. Don't fuss now, don't fuss. It's all right.

SIBYL

(*Burying her face in her mother's arms*)

I don't feel well, Mummy. Can I go and lie down?

MRS. RAILTON-BELL

Of course you can, dear. We can go into the writing room. Such a
nice comfy sofa, and there's never anyone there. (*She leads her to the*

141

hall door) And don't fret any more, my dear. Try and forget the whole nasty business. Make believe it never happened—that there never was such a person as Major Pollock. That's the way.

(*They disappear together into the hall.*)

LADY MATHESON

She should never have told her like that. It was such a mistake.

CHARLES

(*Angrily*)

I agree. If that girl doesn't end as a mental case it won't be the fault of her mother.

LADY MATHESON

(*Loyally*)

Mr. Stratton—I must say I consider that a quite outrageous way of twisting my remark. I used the word "mistake," and you have no right—

CHARLES

No, I haven't. I'm sorry. The comment was purely my own.

JEAN

It was *your* fault for asking her views.

CHARLES

She was sitting there quite peacefully, apparently listening. I wasn't to know she was in a state of high, suppressed hysteria. I might, admittedly, have guessed, but anyway, I had an idiotic but well-meaning hope that I might get her—just this once—just this once in the whole of her life—to disagree publicly with her mother. It could save her soul if she ever did.

MR. FOWLER

I didn't realize that modern psychiatry recognized so old-fashioned and sentimental a term as soul, Mr. Stratton.

CHARLES

Very well, for "soul" read "mind," and one day when you have a spare ten minutes, explain to me the difference.

MR. FOWLER

I will.

CHARLES

(*Getting up*)

Not now, I'm afraid. It might muddle my anatomical studies. (*To* JEAN) Are you coming?

(JEAN *gets up, rather reluctantly.*)

JEAN

I don't know what's the matter with you this evening, Charles. You're behaving like an arrogant pompous boor.

CHARLES

You must forgive me. I suppose it's just that I'm feeling a little light-headed at finding myself, on an issue of common humanity, in a minority of one. The sin of spiritual pride, that's called—isn't it, Mr. Fowler?

(*He goes out.* JEAN *comes back from the door.*)

JEAN

(*To the other two*)

He's been overworking, you know. He'll be quite different about all this tomorrow. (*Confidently*) I'll see to that.

(MRS. RAILTON-BELL *comes in.*)

143

MRS. RAILTON-BELL

She's quite all right, now. She always recovers from these little states very quickly. She's resting in the writing room.

LADY MATHESON

Oh, good.

JEAN

I was just apologizing for my husband's behavior, Mrs. Railton-Bell.

MRS. RAILTON-BELL

Thank you, my dear—but what I always say is—we're all of us entitled to our own opinions, however odd and dangerous and distasteful they may sometimes be. (*Briskly*) Now. Shall we all go and see Miss Cooper in a body, or would you rather I acted as your spokesman?
(*It is plain which course she would prefer. After a pause, they begin to murmur diffidently.*)

LADY MATHESON

I think, perhaps, if *you* went, dear—

MR. FOWLER

I don't think a deputation is a good idea—

JEAN

You be our spokesman.

MRS. RAILTON-BELL

Very well. (*She picks up the copy of the newspaper and goes to the door*) I hope you all understand it's a duty I hardly relish.
(*She goes out.*)

MR. FOWLER

(*To* LADY MATHESON)

I would hardly call that a strictly accurate self-appraisal, would you?

LADY MATHESON

(*Doubtfully*)

Well—after all— doing a duty can seem a pleasure, to some people, can't it? It never has done to me, I agree, but then I'm—well so weak and silly about these things—

JEAN

(*At the door*)

It would be a pleasure to me in this case. Horrid old man! (*To herself as she goes*) I hope the baby's not been crying—
(*She goes out.*)

MR. FOWLER

A ruthless young girl, that, I would say.

LADY MATHESON

So many young people are these days, don't you think?

MR. FOWLER

(*Meaningly*)

Not only young people.

LADY MATHESON

(*Unhappily*)

Yes—well. (*With a sigh*) Oh, dear! What a dreadful affair. It's made me quite miserable.

MR. FOWLER

I feel a little unhappy about it all myself. (*He sighs and gets up*)

trouble about being on the side of right, as one sees it, is that one sometimes finds oneself in the company of such very questionable allies. Let's go and take our minds off it all with television.

LADY MATHESON

(*Getting up*)

Yes. Good idea. The newsreel will be nearly over now—but I think that dear Philip Harben is on, after. Such a pity I'll never have the chance of following any of his recipes.

MR. FOWLER

(*As they go out*)

I agree. One suffers the tortures of Tantalus, and yet the pleasure is intense. Isn't that what is today called masochism?

(*They go out. The room is empty for a moment, and then* MAJOR POLLOCK *tentatively appears at the open French windows. He peers cautiously into the room, and, satisfying himself that it is empty, comes in. He goes quickly to the table on which are* MRS. RAILTON-BELL's *journals. He sees at once that the* West Hampshire Weekly News *is no longer where he left it. Frantically he rummages through the pile, and then begins to search the room. He is standing, in doubt, by the fireplace, when the door opens quietly and* SIBYL *comes in. As she sees him she stands stock still. He does not move either.*)

MAJOR POLLOCK

(*At length, with pathetic jauntiness*)

Evening, Miss R.B. And how's the world with you, eh?

SIBYL

Were you looking for Mummy's paper?

MAJOR POLLOCK

What? No, of course not. I've got the other copy—

SIBYL

Don't pretend any more, please. She's read it, you see.

MAJOR POLLOCK

Oh. (*There is a long pause. The* MAJOR's *shoulders droop, and he holds the table for support*) Did she show it to you?

SIBYL

Yes.

MAJOR POLLOCK

Oh.

SIBYL

And to all the others.

MAJOR POLLOCK

Miss Cooper too?

SIBYL

Mummy's gone to tell her.
     (*The* MAJOR *nods, hopelessly.*)

MAJOR POLLOCK
(*At length*)

Well—that's it, then, isn't it?

SIBYL

Yes.

MAJOR POLLOCK

Oh, God!
(*He sits down, staring at the floor. She looks at him steadily.*)

SIBYL
(*Passionately*)
Why did you do it? Why did you do it?

MAJOR POLLOCK

I don't know. I wish I could answer that. Why does anyone do anything they shouldn't? Why do some people drink too much, and other
people smoke fifty cigarettes a day? Because they can't stop it, I suppose.

SIBYL

Then this wasn't—the first time?

MAJOR POLLOCK
(*Quietly*)

No.

SIBYL

It's horrible.

MAJOR POLLOCK

Yes, of course it is. I'm not trying to defend it. You wouldn't guess,
I know, but ever since school I've always been scared to death of women.
Of everyone, in a way, I suppose, but mostly of women. I had a bad time
at school—which wasn't Wellington, of course—just a Council school.
Boys hate other boys to be timid and shy, and they gave it to me good
and proper. My father despised me, too. He was a sergeant-major in the
Black Watch. He made me join the Army, but I was always a bitter dis-
appointment to him. He died before I got my commission. I only got that

by a wangle. It wasn't difficult at the beginning of the war. But it meant everything to me, all the same. Being saluted, being called sir— I thought, I'm someone, now, a real person. Perhaps some woman might even—(*He stops*) But it didn't work. It never has worked. I'm made in a certain way, and I can't change it. It has to be the dark, you see, and strangers, because—

SIBYL
(*Holding her hands to her ears*)
Stop, stop. I don't want to hear it. It makes me ill.

MAJOR POLLOCK
(*Quietly*)
Yes. It would, of course. I should have known that. It was only that you'd asked me about why I did such things, and I wanted to talk to someone about it. I never have, you see, not in the whole of my life. (*He gets up and gently touches her sleeve*) I'm sorry to upset *you*, of all people.
(*He goes to a table and collects two books.*)

SIBYL
Why me, so especially? Why not the others?

MAJOR POLLOCK
Oh, I don't give a hang about the others. They'll all take it in their various ways, I suppose—but it won't mean much more to them than another bit of gossip to snort or snigger about. But it'll be different for you, Sibyl, and that makes me unhappy.

SIBYL
That's the first time you've ever called me Sibyl.

MAJOR POLLOCK

Is it? Well, there's not much point in all that Miss R.B. stuff now, is there?

SIBYL

What makes me so different from the others?
(*The* MAJOR *has gathered another book from a corner of the room, and a pipe. He turns now and looks at her.*)

MAJOR POLLOCK

Your being so scared of—well—shall we call it life? It sounds more respectable than the word which I know you hate. You and I are awfully alike, you know. That's why I suppose we've drifted so much together in this place.

SIBYL

How can you say we're alike? *I* don't—
(*She stops, unable to continue.*)

MAJOR POLLOCK

I know you don't. You're not even tempted and never will be. You're very lucky. Or are you? Who's to say, really? All I meant was that we're both of us frightened of people, and yet we've somehow managed to forget our fright when we've been in each other's company. Speaking for myself, I'm grateful and always will be. Of course I can't expect *you* to feel the same way now.

SIBYL

What are you doing?

MAJOR POLLOCK

Getting my things together. Have you seen a pouch anywhere?

SIBYL

It's here.

(*She goes to a table and collects it. He takes it from her.*)

MAJOR POLLOCK

(*With a wry smile*)

Old Wellingtonian colors.

SIBYL

Why have you told so many awful lies?

MAJOR POLLOCK

I don't like myself as I am, I suppose, so I've had to invent another person. It's not so harmful, really. We've all got daydreams. Mine have gone a step further than most people's—that's all. Quite often I've even managed to believe in the Major myself. (*He starts*) Is that someone in the hall?

SIBYL

(*Listening*)

No, I don't think so. Where will you go?

MAJOR POLLOCK

I don't know. There's a chap in London might put me up for a day or two. Only I don't so awfully want to go there—

SIBYL

Why not?

MAJOR POLLOCK

(*After a slight pause*)

Well—you see—it's rather a case of birds of a feather.

SIBYL

Don't go to him. You musn't go to him.

MAJOR POLLOCK

I don't know where else.

SIBYL

Another hotel.

MAJOR POLLOCK

It can't be Bournemouth or anywhere near here. It'll have to be London, and I don't know anywhere there I can afford—

SIBYL

I'll lend you some money.

MAJOR POLLOCK

You certainly won't.

SIBYL

I will. I have some savings certificates. You can have those. I can get more too, if you need it.

MAJOR POLLOCK

(*Holding her hand, gently*)

No, Sibyl. No. Thank you—but no.

SIBYL

But you'll go to this man.

MAJOR POLLOCK

No, I won't. I'll find somewhere else.

SIBYL

Where?

MAJOR POLLOCK

Don't worry. I'll be all right.
(MISS COOPER *comes in, and closes the door behind her.*)

MISS COOPER

(*Brightly*)

There you are, Major Pollock. Can I see you in my office a moment?

MAJOR POLLOCK

We don't need to talk in your office, Miss Cooper. I know what you
have to say. I'm leaving at once.

MISS COOPER

I see. That's your own choice, is it?

MAJOR POLLOCK

Of course.

MISS COOPER

Because I would like to make it perfectly plain to you that there's
no question whatever of my requiring you to leave this hotel. If you
want to stay on here you're at perfect liberty to do so. It's entirely a
matter for you.
(*Pause.*)

MAJOR POLLOCK

I see. That's good of you. But of course I have to go.

MISS COOPER

I quite understand that you'd want to. I shan't charge the usual week's notice. When will you be going? Before dinner?

MAJOR POLLOCK

Of course.

MISS COOPER

Do you want me to help you find some place to stay until you can get settled?

MAJOR POLLOCK

I can hardly expect that, Miss Cooper.

MISS COOPER

Why on earth not? There are two hotels in London run by the Beauregard group. One is in West Kensington and the other in St. John's Wood. They're both about the same price. Which would you prefer?

MAJOR POLLOCK
(*After a pause*)

West Kensington, I think.

MISS COOPER

I've got their card here somewhere. Yes, there's one here. (*She goes to the mantelpiece and takes a card from a small holder. She hands it to him*) Would you like me to ring them up for you?

MAJOR POLLOCK

Thank you, but I think perhaps I'd better ring them myself. In case of—further trouble, I don't want to involve you more than I need. May I use the phone in your office?

154

MISS COOPER

Certainly.

MAJOR POLLOCK

I'll pay for the call, of course. (*He goes to the door and looks to see if anyone is about in the hall*) Sibyl, if I don't have a chance of seeing you again, I'll write and say good-bye.

(*He goes out.* MISS COOPER *turns to* SIBYL.)

MISS COOPER

Your mother's gone up to dress for dinner, Miss Railton-Bell. She told me I'd find you in the writing room lying down and I was to tell you that you can have your meal upstairs tonight, if you'd rather.

SIBYL

That's all right.

MISS COOPER
(*Sympathetically*)

How are you feeling now?

SIBYL
(*Brusquely*)

All right.

(MISS COOPER *approaches her*.)

MISS COOPER
(*Quietly*)

Is there anything I can do to help you?

SIBYL
(*Angrily*)

No. Nothing. And please don't say things like that. You'll make me feel bad again, and I'll make a fool of myself. I feel well now. He's going and that's good. I despise him.

MISS COOPER

Do you? I wonder if you should.

SIBYL

He's a vile, wicked man, and he's done a horrible beastly thing. It's not the first time, either. He admits that.

MISS COOPER

I didn't think it was.

SIBYL

And yet you told him he could stay on in the hotel if he wanted to? 'That's wicked too.

MISS COOPER

Then I suppose I *am* wicked too. (*She puts her hand on her arm*) Sibyl, dear—

SIBYL

Why is everyone calling me Sibyl this evening? Please stop. You'll only make me cry.

MISS COOPER

I don't mean to do that. I just mean to help you. (SIBYL *breaks down suddenly, but now quietly and without hysteria.* MISS COOPER *holds her*) That's better. Much better.

SIBYL

It's so horrible.

MISS COOPER

I know it is. I'm very sorry for you.

SIBYL

He says we're alike—he and I.

MISS COOPER

Does he?

SIBYL

He says we're both scared of life and people and sex. There—I've said the word. He says I hate *saying* it even, and he's right. I do. What's the matter with me? There must be something the matter with me.

MISS COOPER

Nothing very much, I should say. Shall we sit down?
(*She gently propels her on to the sofa and sits beside her.*)

SIBYL

I'm a freak, aren't I?

MISS COOPER

(*In matter-of-fact tones*)
I never know what that word means. If you mean you're different from other people, then, I suppose, you are a freak. But all human beings are a bit different from each other, aren't they? What a dull world it would be if they weren't.

SIBYL

I'd like to be ordinary.

MISS COOPER

I wouldn't know about that, dear. You see, I've never met an ordinary person. To me all people are extraordinary. I meet all sorts here, you know, in my job, and the one thing I've learnt in five years is that the word normal, applied to any human being, is utterly meaningless. In a sort of a way it's an insult to our Maker, don't you think, to suppose that He could possibly work to any set pattern.

SIBYL

I don't think Mummy would agree with you.

MISS COOPER

I'm fairly sure she wouldn't. Tell me—when did your father die?

SIBYL

When I was seven.

MISS COOPER

Did you go to school?

SIBYL

No. Mummy said I was too delicate. I had a governess some of the time, but most of the time Mummy taught me herself.

MISS COOPER

Yes. I see. And you've never really been away from her, have you?

SIBYL

Only when I had a job, for a bit. (*Proudly*) I was a salesgirl in a big shop in London—Jones & Jones. I sold lampshades. But I got ill, though, and had to leave.

MISS COOPER
(*Brightly*)
What bad luck. Well, you must try again, some day, mustn't you?

SIBYL
Mummy says no.

MISS COOPER
Mummy says no. Well, then, you must just try and get Mummy to say yes, don't you think?

SIBYL
I don't know how.

MISS COOPER
I'll tell you how. By running off and getting a job on your own. She'll say yes quick enough then. (*She pats* SIBYL's *knee sympathetically and gets up*) I have my menus to do.
(*She goes towards the door.*)

SIBYL
(*Urgently*)
Will he be all right, do you think?

MISS COOPER
The Major? I don't know. I hope so.

SIBYL

In spite of what he's done, I don't want anything bad to happen to him. I want him to be happy. Is it a nice hotel—this one in West Kensington?

MISS COOPER

Very nice.

SIBYL

Do you think he'll find a friend there? He told me just now that he'd always be grateful to me for making him forget how frightened he was of people.

MISS COOPER

He's helped you too, hasn't he?

SIBYL

Yes.

MISS COOPER
(*After a pause*)

I hope he'll find a friend in the new hotel.

SIBYL

So do I. Oh, God, so do I.
(*The* MAJOR *comes in.*)

MAJOR POLLOCK
(*Quickly, to* MISS COOPER)

It's all right. I've fixed it. It might please you to know that I said *Mr.* Pollock, and didn't have to mention your name, or this hotel. I must dash upstairs and pack now. (*He turns to* SIBYL *and holds out his hand*) Good-bye, Sibyl.

(SIBYL *takes his hand, after a second's hesitation.*)

SIBYL

Good-bye. (*She drops his hand and runs quickly to the door. Without looking back*) God bless you.

(*She goes out.*)

MAJOR POLLOCK

Very upset? (MISS COOPER *nods*) That's the part I've hated most, you know. It's funny. She's rather an odd one—almost a case—she's got a child's mind and hardly makes sense sometimes—and yet she means quite a lot to me.

MISS COOPER

I think you mean quite a lot to her too.

MAJOR POLLOCK

I did, I think. Not now, of course. It was the gallant ex-soldier she was fond of—not—(*He stops*) I told her the whole story about myself. I thought it right. There's just a chance she might understand it all a bit better one day. I'm afraid, though, she'll never get over it.

MISS COOPER

No. I don't suppose she will.

MAJOR POLLOCK

One's apt to excuse oneself sometimes by saying, well, after all, what I do doesn't do anybody much harm. But one does, you see. That's not a thought I like. Could you have a squint in the hall and see if anyone's around?

(MISS COOPER *half opens the door.*)

MISS COOPER

Miss Meacham's at the telephone.

MAJOR POLLOCK

Damn.

MISS COOPER

What train are you catching?

MAJOR POLLOCK

Seven forty-five.

MISS COOPER

You've got time.

MAJOR POLLOCK

I've got a tremendous lot of packing to do. Four years, you know. Hellish business. I'm dreading the first few days in a new place. I mean dreading, you know—literally trembling with funk at the thought of meeting new people. The trouble is I'll probably be forced by sheer terror to take refuge in all that Major stuff again.

MISS COOPER

Try not to.

MAJOR POLLOCK

Oh, I'll try all right. I'll try. I only hope I'll succeed. (*He goes cautiously to the door and turns*) Still there. Damn. (*Coming back*)

Thank you for being so kind. God knows why you have been. I don't deserve it—but I'm grateful. Very grateful.

MISS COOPER

That's all right.

MAJOR POLLOCK

You're an odd fish, you know, if you don't mind my saying so. A good deal more goes on behind that calm managerial front of yours than anyone would imagine. Has something bad ever happened to you?

MISS COOPER

Yes.

MAJOR POLLOCK

Very bad?

MISS COOPER

I've got over it.

MAJOR POLLOCK

What was it?

MISS COOPER

I loved a man who loved somebody else.

MAJOR POLLOCK

Still love him?

MISS COOPER

Oh, yes. I always will.

MAJOR POLLOCK

Any hope?

MISS COOPER
(*Cheerfully*)

No. None at all.

MAJOR POLLOCK

Why so cheerful about it?

MISS COOPER

Because there's no point in being anything else. I've settled for the situation, you see, and it's surprising how cheerful one can be when one gives up hope. I've still got the memory, you see, which is a very pleasant one—all things considered.

MAJOR POLLOCK
(*Nodding*)

I see. Quite the philosopher, what? (*To himself*) I must give up saying what. Well, Meacham or no Meacham, I'm going to make a dash for it, or I'll miss that train.
(*He turns back to the door.*)

MISS COOPER

Why don't you stay?

MAJOR POLLOCK
(*Turning, incredulously*)

Stay? In the hotel, you mean?

MISS COOPER

You say you dread the new hotel.

164

MAJOR POLLOCK

I dread this one a damn sight more, now.

MISS COOPER

Yes, I expect you do. But at least you couldn't be forced by terror into any more Major stuff, could you?
(*Pause.*)

MAJOR POLLOCK

I might be forced into something a good deal more—conclusive—cleaning my old service revolver, perhaps—you know the form—make a nasty mess on one of your carpets and an ugly scandal in your hotel.

MISS COOPER
(*Lightly*)

I'd take the risk, if you would.

MAJOR POLLOCK

My dear Miss Cooper, I'm far too much of a coward to stay on here now. Far too much.

MISS COOPER

I see. Pity. I just thought it would be so nice if you could prove to yourself that you weren't.
(*Pause.*)

MAJOR POLLOCK
(*At length*)

You're thinking of her too, of course, aren't you?

MISS COOPER

Yes.

MAJOR POLLOCK

Reinstate the gallant ex-soldier in her eyes?

MISS COOPER

That's right.

MAJOR POLLOCK

Make her think she's helped me find my soul and all that.

MISS COOPER

Yes.
(*Another pause.*)

MAJOR POLLOCK
(*With an eventual sigh*)

Not a hope. Not a hope in the whole, wide, blinking world. I know my form, you see.

MISS COOPER

I wonder if you do.

MAJOR POLLOCK
(*Sadly*)

Oh, I do. I do, only too well. Thanks for trying, anyway. (*He looks cautiously out into the hall*) Coast's clear. (*He turns round and looks at her for a long time. She stares back steadily at him. He speaks again, at length*) There's a nine-something train, isn't there?

MISS COOPER

Nine thirty-two.
(*There is another pause as he looks at her in doubt. Then he gives a shamefaced smile.*)

MAJOR POLLOCK

I expect I'll still catch the seven forty-five.
  (*He goes out.*)

The Lights Fade

Scene II

The dining room. As at the beginning of the first play, dinner is in full swing. The table by the window is now occupied by a pair of young "casuals"—much interested in each other, and totally oblivious of everyone else. One table is unoccupied and unset; otherwise all the tables are occupied by the usual owners.

As the lights come on, conversation is general—which means, more precisely, that the two casuals are murmuring together, the STRATTONS *are arguing,* LADY MATHESON *and* MR. FOWLER *are talking between tables, and* MRS. RAILTON-BELL *is talking to* SIBYL. MABEL *is hovering over* MISS MEACHAM, *who is absorbed in* Racing Up to Date.

MABEL

(Heard above the background)

Were you the fricassee or the Cambridge steak?

MISS MEACHAM

What? Oh, it doesn't matter. Both are uneatable.

MABEL

What about the cold chicken, then?

MISS MEACHAM

Cold chicken? But we haven't had it hot yet.

MABEL

If I were you I'd have the fricassee. It's all right. It's rabbit.

MISS MEACHAM

The fricassee then.

MR. FOWLER

Any cheese, Mabel?

MABEL

Afraid not.

MR. FOWLER

There's never any cheese.
(MABEL *serves* MRS. MEACHAM *and stumps out to the kitchen.*
MRS. RAILTON-BELL *leans across to* LADY MATHESON.)

MRS. RAILTON-BELL

I believe there's a new game on television tonight.

LADY MATHESON

Yes. I know, dear. I read all about it in the *Radio Times*. It sounds
quite fascinating—I shall certainly see it next week.

MRS. RAILTON-BELL

Why not tonight, hear?

LADY MATHESON

I feel too tired. I'm going to go to bed directly after dinner.

MRS. RAILTON-BELL

Of course. (*Lowering her voice*) What a really nerve-racking day
it's been, hasn't it? I don't suppose any of us will ever forget it. Ever. I
feel utterly shattered, myself. (*To* SIBYL) Pass the sauce, dear.

(LADY MATHESON *nods.* MRS. RAILTON-BELL *takes a sip of wine. The* MAJOR *has walked quietly into the dining room.* MRS. RAILTON-BELL *turns and stares unbelievingly at him as he walks slowly to his table and sits down. The conversation in the dining room has frozen into a dead silence, for even "the casuals" seem affected by the electric atmosphere—though oblivious of the cause—and have ceased talking. The silence is broken by* DOREEN *entering the dining room and seeing him.*)

DOREEN

(*Calling through the kitchen door*)
Mabel—Number Seven's in. You said he was out.

MABEL

(*Off*)
Well, that's what Joe said. Joe said he was leaving before dinner.

DOREEN

Sorry, Major. There's been a muddle. I'll lay your table right away. (*She goes back into the kitchen. The silence remains unbroken, until* DOREEN *returns with a tray and begins quickly to set the* MAJOR's *table*) What would you like? The fricassee's nice.

MAJOR POLLOCK

I'll have that. Thank you.

DOREEN

Soup first?

MAJOR POLLOCK

No, thank you.

170

DOREEN

(*Finally setting the table*)

There we are. All cosy now. Fricassee, you said?

MAJOR POLLOCK

That's right.

(*She goes into the kitchen.* SIBYL *is staring at the* MAJOR, *but he does not meet her eyes. He is looking down at his table, as is everyone else, aware of his presence, save* SIBYL *and* MRS. RAILTON-BELL, *who is glaring furiously in turn at him and at the others. The silence is broken suddenly by a rather nervously high-pitched greeting from* CHARLES.)

CHARLES

(*To the* MAJOR)

Hullo.

MAJOR POLLOCK

(*Murmuring*)

Hullo.

CHARLES

Clouding over a bit, isn't it? I'm afraid we may get rain later.

(JEAN *is furiously glaring at her husband.* MRS. RAILTON-BELL *has turned fully round in her chair in an attempt to paralyze him into silence.*)

MAJOR POLLOCK

Yes. I'm afraid we may.

MISS MEACHAM

We need it. This hard going's murder on form. (*To* MAJOR POLLOCK) You know Newmarket, don't you?

MAJOR POLLOCK

No, I don't.

MISS MEACHAM

But I remember your saying—(*She gets it*) Oh, I see. Well, it's a very tricky course in hard going. Still if they get some rain up there to-morrow, I think I'll be able to give you a winner on Tuesday.

MAJOR POLLOCK

Thank you. Thank you very much. The only thing is, I may not be here on Tuesday.

MISS MEACHAM

Oh, really? All right. Leave me your address then and I'll wire it to you. I'll need the money for the wire, though.

MAJOR POLLOCK

Thank you. That's very kind of you.

MISS MEACHAM

You won't think it so kind of me, if it loses.
(*She goes back to her* Racing Up to Date. MISS COOPER *comes in.*)

MISS COOPER

(*Brightly*)

Good evening, Mrs. Railton-Bell. Good evening, Lady Matheson. Good evening, Mr. Pollock. (*The "Mr." is barely distinguishable from "Major," and her voice is as brightly "managerial" to him as to the others*) I hear they didn't lay your table tonight. I'm so sorry.

MAJOR POLLOCK

Quite all right.

MISS COOPER

I'd advise the fricassee, if I were you. It's really awfully nice.

MAJOR POLLOCK

I've ordered it.

MISS COOPER

Good, I'm so glad. (*She passes on*) Good evening, Mr. and Mrs Stratton. Everything all right? (*They nod and smile*) Splendid.
(*She bows rather less warmly to "the casuals" and goes out.* MRS. RAILTON-BELL *pretends to feel an imaginary draught.*)

MRS. RAILTON-BELL
(*To* LADY MATHESON)

It's very cold in here suddenly, don't you think, dear? (LADY MATHE-SON *nods, nervously*) I'll think I'll turn my chair round a bit, and get out of the draught.
(*She does so, turning her back neatly on the* MAJOR. MR. FOWLER *gets up quietly from his table and walks to the door. To do this he has to pass the* MAJOR. *A step or so past him he hesitates and then looks back, nods and smiles.*)

MR. FOWLER

Good evening.

MAJOR POLLOCK

Good evening.
(MRS. RAILTON-BELL *has had to twist her head sharply round in order to allow her eyes to confirm this shameful betrayal.*)

173

MR. FOWLER

Hampshire did pretty well today, did you see? Three hundred and eighty-odd for five.

MAJOR POLLOCK

Very good.

MR. FOWLER

I wish they had more bowling. Well—
(*He smiles vaguely and goes on into the lounge. There is an audible and outraged "Well!" from* MRS. RAILTON-BELL. *Silence falls again. Suddenly and by an accident the* MAJOR'S *and* LADY MATHESON'S *eyes meet. Automatically she inclines her head and gives him a slight smile. He returns the salute.*)

LADY MATHESON
(*To* MAJOR POLLOCK)

Good evening.

MRS. RAILTON-BELL
(*In a whisper*)

Gladys!
(LADY MATHESON, *who has genuinely acted from instinct, looks startled. Then she apparently decides to be as well hanged for a sheep as a lamb.*)

LADY MATHESON
(*Suddenly very bold, and in a loud voice*)

I advise the apple charlotte. It's very good.

MAJOR POLLOCK

Thank you. I'll have that.
(*She is instantly conscience-stricken at what she has done and hangs her head over her apple charlotte, eating feverishly. She*

refuses to look at MRS. RAILTON-BELL, *who is staring at her with wide, unbelieving and furious eyes.* MRS. RAILTON-BELL, *getting no response from* LADY MATHESON, *deliberately folds her napkin and rises.*

MRS. RAILTON-BELL
(Quietly)

Come, Sibyl.

SIBYL
(Equally quietly)

I haven't finished yet, Mummy.

MRS. RAILTON-BELL
(Looking puzzled at this unaccustomed response)

It doesn't matter, dear. Come into the lounge.
> (SIBYL *makes no move to rise. She stares up at her mother. There is a pause.*)

SIBYL

No, Mummy.
> (*Pause.*)

MRS. RAILTON-BELL
(Sharply)

Sibyl, come with me at once—

SIBYL
(With quiet firmness)

No, Mummy. I'm going to stay in the dining room, and finish my dinner. (MRS. RAILTON-BELL *hesitates, plainly meditating various courses of action. Finally she decides on the only really possible course*

175

left to her—the dignified exit. Before she has got to the door SIBYL *has spoken to the* MAJOR) There's a new moon tonight, you know. We must all go and look at it afterwards.

MAJOR POLLOCK

Yes. We must.

> (DOREEN *has bustled in with the* MAJOR'S *dish as* MRS. RAIL-TON-BELL, *her world crumbling, goes into the lounge.* DOREEN *serves* MAJOR POLLOCK.)

DOREEN

Sorry it's been so long. You're a bit late, you see.

MAJOR POLLOCK

Yes. My fault.

DOREEN

What's the matter with you tonight? You always say *"mea culpa."* (*She beats her breast in imitation of an obvious* MAJOR *bon mot.*)

MAJOR POLLOCK

Do I? Well—they both mean the same, don't they?

DOREEN

I suppose so. (*Finishing the serving*) There you are. Now what about breakfast?

MAJOR POLLOCK

Breakfast?

176

DOREEN

Joe got it wrong about your going, didn't he?
  (*There is a pause.* SIBYL *is looking steadily at the* MAJOR, *who now raises his eyes from his plate and meets her glance.*)

MAJOR POLLOCK
  (*Quietly, at length*)

Yes, he did.

DOREEN

That's good. Breakfast usual time, then?

MAJOR POLLOCK

Yes, Doreen. Breakfast usual time.
  (DOREEN *goes into the kitchen.* MAJOR POLLOCK *begins to eat his fricassee.* SIBYL *continues to eat her sweet. A decorous silence, broken only by the renewed murmur of "the casuals," reigns once more, and the dining room of the Beauregard Private Hotel no longer gives any sign of the battle that has just been fought and won between its four bare walls.*)

Curtain